PRAISE FOR
LEAD WITH FAITH, PLAY WITH PURPOSE

Lead with Faith, Play with Purpose is a faith-filled guide where athletes of all ages can find timeless principles, practical methods, and, most importantly, the person of God on every page.

Jonathan Rainey, pastor, Seattle Seahawks

I remember what it was like to be a college basketball player—fighting to stay afloat in the classroom, battling for success on the hardwood, navigating challenging relationships, and struggling to give God dedicated time in my day-to-day grind. I needed meaningful, accessible injections of hope rooted in Scripture and applicable to my life, and that is precisely what Andy Dooley provides in this book. His winsome voice is always a gift, and I'm thrilled that the athletes I serve will benefit from the timely words of a man who has walked in their shoes and has left footsteps worth following in.

Brian McCormack, executive director,
Breakaway Ministries, Texas A&M University

A huge shoutout to Andy Dooley for answering the call to do this project. Join me and others who lead by faith in reading this devotional book packed with testimonies, prayers, and Scripture. You will be challenged to go deeper into God's Word and encouraged to play with purpose.

Johnny Shelton, chaplain/spiritual adviser,
Baltimore Ravens; founder, Attitudes In Motion, Inc.

In *Lead with Faith, Play with Purpose*, Andy Dooley uses his life experiences to give a captivating glimpse into the locker room of an athlete's journey toward building their faith. Through a blend of Scripture, prayer, and practical application, he provides a compelling playbook for athletes and coaches who want to deepen their relationship with Christ. In insightful and empowering ways, Andy identifies the importance of addressing the emotional, relational, and spiritual dimensions of an athlete's life. We need more leaders like Andy whose passion is to guide athletes to live lives of purpose both on and off the field.

Kevin L. Nickerson, founder, GameBreakers
Academy; chaplain, Los Angeles Rams

LEAD *WITH* FAITH, PLAY *WITH* PURPOSE

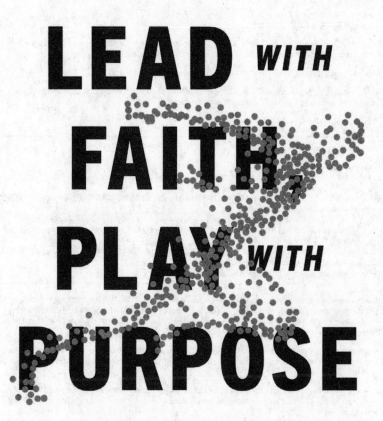

LEAD WITH FAITH

PLAY WITH PURPOSE

A 100-DAY DEVOTIONAL
FOR ATHLETES

ANDY DOOLEY

**ZONDERVAN
BOOKS**

ZONDERVAN BOOKS

Lead with Faith, Play with Purpose
Copyright © 2024 by Andy L. Dooley

Published in Grand Rapids, Michigan, by Zondervan. Zondervan is a registered trademark of The Zondervan Corporation, L.L.C., a wholly owned subsidiary of HarperCollins Christian Publishing, Inc.

Requests for information should be addressed to customercare@harpercollins.com.

Zondervan titles may be purchased in bulk for educational, business, fundraising, or sales promotional use. For information, please email SpecialMarkets@Zondervan.com.

ISBN 978-0-310-36793-2 (audio)

Library of Congress Cataloging-in-Publication Data

Names: Dooley, Andy, 1980- author.
Title: Lead with faith, play with purpose : a 100-day devotional for athletes / Andy Dooley.
Description: Grand Rapids, Michigan : Zondervan Books, 2024.
Identifiers: LCCN 2023057799 (print) | LCCN 2023057800 (ebook) | ISBN 9780310367918 (trade paperback) | ISBN 9780310367925 (ebook)
Subjects: LCSH: Athletes—Prayers and devotions. | Athletes—Religious life. | Sports—Religious aspects—Christianity. | BISAC: RELIGION / Christian Living / Devotional | RELIGION / Christian Living / Spiritual Growth
Classification: LCC BV4596.A8 D66 2024 (print) | LCC BV4596.A8 (ebook) | DDC 242/.68—dc23/eng/20240314
LC record available at https://lccn.loc.gov/2023057799
LC ebook record available at https://lccn.loc.gov/2023057800

Cover design: Micah Kandros
Cover illustrations: Login / oksanka007 / Shutterstock
Interior design: Denise Froehlich

Printed in the United States of America

24 25 26 27 28 LBC 5 4 3 2 1

To my beautiful family of athletes
who inspire me every day to work harder—
Tiffany, Hope, Skylee, Andy II, and Ava—
you have given me the drive
to love God more, be great, and bless others.

―――――――――――

And to my fellow athletes all over the world
who encounter everything
that comes with being an athlete—
I pray that this book will be a cheat code
to navigate through the different seasons
of your athletic career and beyond
as faith-filled leaders.

CONTENTS

There are many obstacles you face as an athlete, and if you don't have a solid foundation it will feel as if you are living life on a small boat trying to sail alone through the Indian Ocean. As an athlete, a coach, and a dad of athletes, I've come to realize that our gifts, talents, and influence are not our own. They don't belong to us; they belong to the one who created us and loves us and has a plan for us. The sooner we recognize this, the better positioned we are to stay connected to God and to be used by him for his greater purposes.

Being an athlete today is hard—and every athlete, no matter what level they compete at, needs support, encouragement, and guidance. It's no secret that collegiate and professional athletes have many distractions and people charming them and competing for a spot in their circle. The freedom and privileges these athletes experience can make it hard for them to stay focused. If you are a younger athlete, know that the sports world has changed drastically, and you may start to experience similar distractions and pressures early on in your athletic career.

The stress athletes are under ranges from trying to satisfy their families, coaches, teammates, and the media, to dealing with the ongoing pressure to improve and excel in their sport—including winning championships and setting records—as well as the constant struggle for mental stability. All of this is a very heavy load to carry. Unfortunately, the cases of depression, anxiety, and other mental health–related issues are rising rapidly among young athletes, which is what inspired me to create this athlete-focused, interactive devotional, which I hope will guide and encourage you to live a life pleasing to God. The Lord has given each of us a specific plan to carry out. I want to help athletes and those who influence them to work toward a healthier mindset and a closer walk with God as they find peace, rely on their heavenly Father for protection, and discover ways to use their own influence to help change the world for good.

This devotional is for everyone who competes in any kind of sports or athletics—and for anyone who coaches, trains, mentors, or leads athletes. You can use it alone, one-on-one with a mentor or a teammate, or with an entire team or small group. Each devotional consists of five parts—a helpful verse or verses from Scripture about the day's topic; a series of "pre-game" questions to get you focused and thinking; an inspiring "game time" devotional message that helps you apply God's Word to your own life and situation; a prayer to ask God for his help in applying the lesson to daily life; and several "postgame keys" that equip you to practice what you've learned.

Now, let's play!

1   UNITY OVER DIVISION

I appeal to you, brothers and sisters, in the name of our
Lord Jesus Christ, that all of you agree with one another in
what you say and that there be no divisions among you,
but that you be perfectly united in mind and thought.
1 CORINTHIANS 1:10

PREGAME

Do you feel like your team is united or divided? Do you ever find yourself in disagreements with your teammates or coaches? Are there teammates you don't like or particularly enjoy being around? Do you have a certain teammate who always creates division between players?

GAME TIME

It can be difficult at times to be a part of a team. Everyone comes from different backgrounds, cultures, and beliefs. You connect with and build good team chemistry with some teammates right away, and then there are those who take work to be around—let alone working together with them for a common goal. I remember my freshman year in college, I had instant connections with many of my football teammates. However, I didn't vibe with a few, and some of them didn't like me either, including a few older guys who wanted to make sure I earned my spot and felt the need to constantly remind me of their status as upperclassmen.

Some of my teammates and I never clicked. One particular teammate broke an unwritten rule and tried to air our beef and tension outside of the locker room. In fact, he attempted to spread it throughout the entire campus. This was unheard of. You could argue, fight, and have disagreements within the locker room walls, and as brothers you would work it out. But you never, ever took it public. That intensified my disdain for my teammate so much that I wanted to harm him. But at the same time, I heard a strong voice in my head telling me, *It's not worth it*. God also sent another teammate to talk to me right before I went to encounter this difficult teammate and commit an act I would have later regretted. God spoke through my friend, who told me exactly what I needed to hear at that very moment.

Although I listened to God and controlled my actions, there still wasn't unity between my teammate and me, and this caused a divide among our team. The tension eventually manifested into a huge argument and near fisticuffs minutes before we took the field on a beautiful fall Saturday afternoon that was perfect for an NCAA football game. It's hard to win when you're not in agreement, united, or willing to battle for each other against your opponents. More importantly, it's tough to be in tune and united with God when you have feelings of anger toward another person.

When Paul talks about unity in the Bible, he isn't saying you can't or won't have disagreements or you have to be someone you're not. We are not robots. We are human beings with differences. However, our goal should always be *unity*. When Paul addressed the Corinthian church, he told them to work together as believers to pursue unity. People playing on the same team can agree to disagree and work together toward a common goal. As believers in Jesus Christ, we should always set our sights on the highest standard. In our every action and decision, Jesus should always be our filter. When we make Jesus the center of every aspect of our lives, we align ourselves with him, and it helps us in our decision-making. Being aligned with Jesus makes us better humans, teammates, friends, sons, and daughters, and it also makes us more coachable athletes who consequently have a greater chance of success.

When every team member is the best version of themselves, they can more efficiently reach their common goals as a team. When Jesus is our common denominator in life, it's hard not to be successful and win.

When you're upset with a teammate or frustrated by a lack of unity on your team, remember to filter your thoughts, actions, and words through Jesus Christ. Remind yourself to pause so you can respond versus react in a situation. As a team, we are always stronger when we prioritize unity over division.

Dear God,
Please help me to fall in love with the desire to be unified with my
teammates, with other believers, and with you. I want to live a life
that reflects you in every area. Instill humility and grace in me so
I can get along with and be a blessing to my coaches and team-
mates. Amen.

POSTGAME KEYS

1. When you're upset, remind yourself to filter your thoughts, actions, and words through Jesus Christ. Memorize 1 Corinthians 1:10 to help you do this.
2. When someone upsets you or disagrees with you, remember to pause so you can respond instead of react.
3. As a team, you are much better unified than divided. Pursue unity by thinking of ways to be a better team player on and off the field or court.

2

TAP IN

The weapons we fight with are not the weapons of the world. On
the contrary, they have divine power to demolish strongholds.
2 CORINTHIANS 10:4

PREGAME

Do you have a pregame go-to? What do you do to prepare for your competitions? What do you do to tap into a different mindset when you need an extra boost? What helps you have an advantage over your opponents? Do you rely on yourself to get through adversity, or do you look to someone else?

In this world, it's easy to believe you are in charge of your life and your destiny. Early on in my sports career, I believed that if I worked hard, learned my sport, studied the playbook, and did the necessary things to get stronger and faster, I would be successful. I think this is because I looked up to professional athletes who were superior in their respective sports, and, unfortunately, I didn't see them give glory to God—they gave all the credit to their own hard work and effort. In the Bible, Paul knew the key to victory was much bigger than simple physical human effort. It's why he said, "The weapons we fight with are not the weapons of the world. On the contrary, they have divine power to demolish strongholds" (2 Corinthians 10:4).

Athletes who can tap into the Lord's divine power through prayer and connecting to the Holy Spirit will have a supernatural edge on their competition. First of all, they know their lives are not their own. These athletes know their talents and giftings come from the Lord. You can be on top today and injured tomorrow. You can be the starter today and on the bench tomorrow. You can be the best athlete at your competition and still suffer defeat. Having the right perspective on who you are and where your talents and giftings come from directly impacts how you live and view life.

In Ephesians 6, Paul clearly describes the word of God and prayer as spiritual weapons: "Finally, be strong in the Lord and in his mighty power. Put on the full armor of God, so that you can take your stand against the devil's schemes. For our struggle is not against flesh and blood, but against the rulers, against the authorities, against the powers of this dark world and against the spiritual forces of evil in the heavenly realms" (verses 10–12). It's not easy trying to battle against others or spiritual forces on your own, but when you're tapped into the Lord, you have an unfair advantage against your opponents.

We all need the power of Jesus on our side. Jesus wants us to rely on him. He wants to come alongside you and give you direction and an advantage. When you doubt yourself, you can give it to the Lord. You can tap into his supernatural peace and healing when you have wicked or self-destructive thoughts, when you deal with anger, or when you are fighting pride and conceit. God is a good God, and he wants the best for you. That's why he provides you with the supernatural cheat code. Don't be afraid to ask him to lead your life in every area.

Today, before practice or even before you start your day, ask God to give you his insight, protection, direction, and strength. Anytime you find yourself wanting to get involved in an argument or feel your pride rising, ask God to intervene and fight your battles as you lay your pride aside and practice humility. Memorize 2 Corinthians 10:4 and recite it when you feel like you need to tap into a supernatural source of strength.

LET'S PRAY

Dear God,
I want to lay my own pride aside and tap into your strength on a regular basis. Teach me how to learn more about who you are, and help me to remember to give you credit for my talents and giftings. Amen.

POSTGAME KEYS

1. Make a daily practice of asking God to give you supernatural insight, protection, direction, and strength.
2. Memorize 2 Corinthians 10:4 and recite it before your practices and competitions.
3. Think of some ways you can lay your pride aside, practice humility, and give credit to others—including God.

WHEN INJURIES VISIT

So do not fear, for I am with you;
do not be dismayed, for I am your God.
I will strengthen you and help you;
I will uphold you with my righteous right hand.
ISAIAH 41:10

Do you worry about getting injured? How do you react when you get hurt? Does your mindset become negative, or do you see adversity as a challenge to be conquered? How does it make you feel when you see someone else get hurt in the same sport that you play?

There is always a wrong time to get injured in athletics. First of all, getting hurt never feels good. No one wants to be in discomfort. Some injuries are worse than losing to your opponent since they can keep you from competing—and practicing—for a while. When you're unable to play or work out, it can mess with your psyche. It can evoke anger, anxiety, depression, and a destructive mindset. Fear can also creep in as you think about the "what if" scenarios: *What if I don't recover fast enough? What if I'm never the same athlete? What if this makes me prone to injury again? What if I lose my position? What if my team cuts me and replaces me, and I'm unable to come back? What if I can't play this sport ever again?*

I dealt with some of these "what ifs" when I was injured in football during my senior year of high school. During the heart of my college recruiting process, I suffered a torn meniscus in my left knee in our season opener. When I found out that I'd be out for six weeks, I was dismal and devastated—but also determined to schedule my surgery quickly and start the rehab process immediately. I was worried college coaches would pull out from the recruiting race, and I would lose my scholarship offers. My mindset went from pain and fear to determination and calling on God for his supernatural help.

In Isaiah 41:10, God lets us know in such a loving way that he has our back and is with us every step. He reminds us not to be fearful and tells us that we can have complete faith in him, as he will hold us up when we feel feeble and weak. We may not be able to walk, but God will walk alongside us.

Getting injured is a trying and tough time in an athlete's life. When you get hurt, don't become a recluse and attempt to battle it on your own.

Injury is the time to dig deeper into God's Word, spend more time with him, and strengthen your faith. Surround yourself with positive people who will speak life into your situation. Did you know that part of your healing process is your mindset and how you see God? You have the choice to see an injury as a major setback or as adversity to overcome and learn from. You serve a good God who promises to have your best interest in mind, and your testimony about this trying time could be the story that helps thousands of people or even just one individual whom God intended to be reached. You never know.

If you're injured, take it one day at a time, listen to the medical professionals, and trust God in the whole process. Because he knows the purpose of this minor setback. And he is preparing you for your comeback.

LET'S PRAY

Dear God,
I ask for quick healing and protection over my mind and body.
Grace me with the patience to endure any setbacks I experience
during my time of recovery from injury and to trust in you. Amen.

POSTGAME KEYS

1. Trust God during times of adversity, knowing he has your best interest at heart.
2. Memorize Isaiah 41:10 or write it down (or print it out) and hang it up where you can see it daily as a reminder that God is faithful.
3. Create a Spiritual First Aid Kit:

   ▶ Write the following Scriptures on note cards: Isaiah 40:29–31; Philippians 3:14; and 1 Timothy 4:12. These will be your go-to when you feel defeated or upset about your circumstances.
   ▶ Make a worship playlist with songs that help you focus on Jesus and all he is and has done for you.
   ▶ Choose a book you believe would be a great read during tough times to help bring your spirits up and center your mind back

on Jesus. (One example would be *The Way of the Warrior* by Erwin Raphael McManus.) Read the book while you're waiting for rehab appointments.

► Purchase your favorite healthy snacks from the grocery store. Eat them before or after rehab sessions to remind yourself to stay strong and healthy.

► Gather all of the above items and put them in your Spiritual First Aid Kit so you're prepared for the adversity of injury. Also, label that playlist on your phone or device so you know what it's for. Now, you're prepared and reminded to not give up on faith, knowing that God always has your back.

4 ATHLETE WITH A PURPOSE

Each of you should use whatever gift you have received to serve others, as faithful stewards of God's grace in its various forms.
1 PETER 4:10

PREGAME

While you're passionate about playing your sport, is it hard to keep your cool sometimes in the heat of competition? Do you ever think about your impact and influence on the people who are watching you participate in the sport you love? Have you ever thought about how you come across to your opponents? What do you think your greater purpose as an athlete is?

GAME TIME

I can tell you firsthand that it won't always be easy to remember to represent God in everything you do on a court, field, or rink; in a pool or ring; or at a match or meet, because the enemy is always trying to find a way to test you and make God look bad. On one particular play in a football game, I was tackled to the ground and lying under a pile of guys. If you are at all claustrophobic, you can imagine it was not a good feeling. When you're in that situation, anxiety can start to creep in, and you are very aware that you're stuck because your opponents and teammates must get up first. Anything can happen to you underneath a pile—gut punches, twisting of extremities, hair tugging, and much more.

While I was at the bottom of the pile in this memorable situation, one of my opponents deliberately stuck his thumb in my face mask and dug it into the side of my cheek. I felt the shearing of the inside of my mouth and tasted the blood while I lay there helpless. I was so mad that all I could think about was what I would do to this player once I got up. When I finally got up, I looked for his jersey number so I could get him back.

But then I remembered what my parents had always told me: "Don't forget that you represent God everywhere." Although I had been done wrong, I knew it wasn't my place to avenge how I had been treated. Deuteronomy 20:4 says, "For the LORD your God is the one who goes with you to fight for you against your enemies to give you victory." Recalling that verse gave me comfort in turning the other cheek, literally, so that I didn't respond in a manner that was all about me.

Having God at the center of your life provides you with security and allows you to see situations from his perspective. When you know to whom you belong and from whom all good things come, you have the freedom to know that life isn't all about you. It's about God. We all play a position on the team God has put together in the body of Christ. Your specific mix of giftings and talents are strategic. Our mentality should be to serve others with the gifts we were given.

How you participate and conduct yourself in your sport represents the God you serve. As believers, our approach to life should differ from how the world suggests we live. We should get excited at any chance to turn the other cheek, represent Jesus, and serve others. As an individual athlete, you can make a powerful difference by showing those who are watching you compete how you handle adversity or victory. Your actions can encourage, empower, and elevate them in their own lives—both on and off the field.

Dear God,
I need you daily. Help me to remember the bigger picture and to
understand that I'm here as your representative in every area of
my life. Remind me to be a light to my teammates, my opponents,
and everyone who is watching me play. Amen.

POSTGAME KEYS

1. Start your day with a prayer, this devotional, or a prayer walk. Doing this consistently will set your day up for success and remind you that God is first in your life.
2. Think of some ways you can choose to represent God in your everyday life.
3. Consider how you represent God in all you do. Remind yourself that focusing on him makes a big difference in your decision making.

5   BRAG ON HIM

Therefore, as it is written: "Let the one who boasts boast in the Lord."
1 CORINTHIANS 1:31

PREGAME

Have you ever witnessed a cocky person talking about themselves and bragging about everything they can do? How does it make you feel to listen to and hang out with someone like that? Does it make you respect that person and want to be like them, or does it make you want to avoid them? Do you feel like that cocky person could sometimes be you?

GAME TIME

I love competition! It energizes me and causes me to perform at a higher level. I lock in and focus that much more because I don't want to lose. I'm also not the one to start the trash talk, but if it occurs, I don't mind finishing it in fun. And I feel an extra boost to win when I'm competing against someone who is cocky, because I know they are at a disadvantage. They think they are above everyone, and they don't give credit to the gift-giver—rather, they believe *they* are the gift. But that's not true at all.

The world will give you a false view of confidence—we might think it builds us up, but in the end, it only breaks us down. We, as humans, love drama. We highlight a cocky athlete and all he or she does in the spotlight; however, as soon as that athlete messes up, the media quickly humiliates them. I watched a young man at a track meet propel out of the starting blocks in a 100-meter race, and while he was running, he was cooking all of his opponents. He was easily a whole person ahead of everyone else. Before he crossed the finish line, he looked back at his opponents and threw up the peace sign. Almost instantaneously it was as if someone threw oil down in his lane. He lost his footing, fell to the ground, and watched in disbelief as everyone else in the race crossed the finish line ahead of him.

I'm sure this young sprinter learned multiple lessons that day. He'd probably seen another athlete pull a similar stunt that ended differently and thought it would be cool to do the same thing; however, it didn't turn out how he envisioned it. In many ways, we can't fault this athlete. We live in a culture where it's okay to put the focus on self. In the Bible, Paul tells us that the Christians in Corinth lived in a similar culture, where there was a lack of humility and little focus on God.

As Christians, we have moral standards, and we need to conduct ourselves with this in mind. Just because we are athletes does not change that we are to live as representatives of God. We live *in* this world; we aren't *of* this world. The more we distance ourselves from consistent communication and connection with God, the easier it becomes to allow the world to seep into our everyday lives and drop our moral standards to fit the world's standards.

If your track coach allowed you to slow down in practice before you crossed the finish line, you would probably lose at the end. The standards we practice with are the standards we compete with. The Bible gives you key standards that will set you up for success and allow you to carry out God's ultimate plan of giving everyone a chance at eternal life. Without God and the Holy Ghost, we are naturally carnal, crude, selfish, sinful, and unruly. When our egos get the best of us and we boast about ourselves, we create a divide between God and ourselves. We can also create division between teammates and other people we are meant to impact. Just because you are competing against someone doesn't mean you can't leave a positive, lasting effect on them through your actions. If you're struggling with cockiness and bragging, here are some important things to remember:

God is the reason you have air in your lungs.
God is the reason you have a special gift in athletics.
God is the reason you are here on this earth.
God is the reason you have the platform you do to impact others.
God is the reason you have a chance to live for eternity in heaven
one day.
It's not by your strength that you play sports.
It's not by your strength that you have a great smile.
It's not by your strength that you were chosen for the team.
It's not by your strength that you are intelligent.
It's all because of God that we get to play the sport we do and be
ambassadors for Christ. It is an awesome privilege we have to
boast in the Lord.

LET'S PRAY

Dear God,
I pray that I always maintain sight of your goodness and mercy. I
don't ever want to forget that you are the gift-giver, and I get to be
used by you for a higher purpose. When I feel myself getting too
cocky or beginning to brag, please help me to brag on you instead.
Amen.

1. Write down the many ways God has been great in your life. Has he helped you through struggles? Made you really good at what you do? Saved you from pain, injury, or a bad situation? Write it down—and give the glory to him.

2. Think of some ways you can start to boast more about the Lord of your life. Write down a list of people you can talk to about how amazing God is.

3. Don't wait until you're holding a trophy to mention God's name. Learn about him, talk about him, and share him with others daily.

6   NO HONOR IN ARGUING

It is to one's honor to avoid strife,
but every fool is quick to quarrel.
PROVERBS 20:3

PREGAME

Have you noticed that games, matches, meets, competitions, and practices can sometimes get intense? Have you ever been in a heated argument at practice, during a game, or at a competition with a teammate, opponent, fan, or coach? Have you ever felt like you needed to prove yourself or defend your point of view—even if it meant getting into an argument?

GAME TIME

I played running back in college, and my freshman year was one of the hardest years of my life. Like other first-year students, I went from the familiarity of living at home with my family and having a particular schedule to moving into a dorm with strangers, away from my comfortable surroundings and friends. I didn't know anyone except my new teammates, with whom I had been doing two-a-days for a few days. This environment is tough. You feel like you have something to prove to everyone because you are a freshman, new to the program, and you want to make a great impression so your peers and coaches like you. Plus, you want to do well so you can find your place on the team and play that season.

One particular day at practice, I was on the scout team, which means you run the plays of your opponents against your own team's starting offense or defense. The starting defense was on the field, and I was on the scout team offense. The coach told me to run the ball at just 50 percent of my speed. When I received the ball to run the play, I did what I'd been told and barely ran through the line. Out of nowhere, I was hit so hard by one of the starting defensive players that I was completely lifted off the turf, and the back of my shoulders was the first part of my body to violently become reacquainted with the turf. Following the hit, the defensive player stood over me and said, "Welcome to college football!" Thankfully, the hit didn't hurt as much as it bruised my ego. I hopped up quickly, and while I didn't hit him, I did give him a piece of my mind by verbally lashing out, which resulted in an argument—and that was definitely not the answer.

Without guidance, God, and grace, it's extremely hard not to always feel stressed in sports. I love how the Christian Standard Bible (CSB) translates Proverbs 20:3: "Honor belongs to the person who ends a dispute, but any fool can get himself into a quarrel." The *honor* in this text means "respect, splendor, glory, reputation." Avoiding conflict and choosing peace are signs of a wise person who has self-control and does not operate foolishly. If I had kept my mouth shut, said nothing, and headed back to the huddle, I would have kept the peace and appeared wise. Instead, I opened my mouth, looked foolish, and lost some respect from my coaches and teammates.

We are not to be hotheads. If we want to be leaders on our teams and in our communities, we must work to remain cool, calm, and collected. This is how Jesus carried himself, and this is how God wants us to be. We are to be promoters of peace, so don't give the devil a chance to cause disruption and division. The more time we spend with God and learning about Jesus, the more we learn how to discern when it's appropriate to engage or disengage from a situation.

LET'S PRAY

Dear God,
Help me to think before I react in a situation that could cause
strife. I want to be a person of wisdom, not foolish actions. Help
me be more like Jesus among my teammates, my opponents, and
everyone I come into contact with. Amen.

POSTGAME KEYS

1. Proverbs 20:3 is a key Scripture that will help you navigate life. Take this week to memorize it so it can be a major part of the soundtrack of your life.
2. This week, take time to notice and be aware of your interactions and emotions when you are in contact with other people. Practice choosing wisdom instead of foolishness.
3. Practice talking to God throughout the day, as you would a friend, and not just at the beginning of your day, at mealtime, or before bed. This will help you have God at the forefront of your mind throughout the day and allow him to guide your responses and actions.

7 CHRISTIAN ATHLETE

"So now I am giving you a new commandment: Love each other.
Just as I have loved you, you should love each other. Your love for
one another will prove to the world that you are my disciples."
JOHN 13:34–35 NLT

Do you ever wonder what it means to be a Christian—let alone a Christian athlete? Do you ever ask yourself if you're in right standing with the Lord? Have you wondered where you will spend eternity once your life on this earth has ended?

I don't know about you, but I used to think about the question of where I would spend eternity quite a bit—and I still take those questions seriously. Typically, when you choose to follow Jesus, you say that you would like to give your life to Christ and then you repeat the sinner's prayer. You make an outward public declaration to live your life for Jesus, and it's truly a powerful moment. It's one of the most important decisions you will ever make in your life.

So often, we have that encounter and experience that moment . . . and then we have no clue what to do next. Questions flood your mind: *How do I act like a Christian? What does it mean to live my life for Christ? Am I good now, since I prayed the sinner's prayer and gave my life to Christ? Does it automatically mean I will enter the gates of heaven? Is it okay to go back to my regular way of living?*

When you decide to live your life for Christ, you declare that you are born again with a new spiritual identity. There should be a change within you that makes you want to live your life like Christ did and desire to get to know who God is. Your old way of living and thinking is transformed and gone; the new is here. You have been born into the family of God, and you desire to live a new life congruent with biblical teachings. However, none of us are perfect, and we make mistakes every day. It can be tough to grow as believers if we don't have any direction or know the next steps to take. If you are fortunate enough to have a spiritual mentor, that is amazing. However, if you don't, I want to help you get on the right course for living a Christian life in your personal life and as an athlete.

First, I want you to find a Bible translation that is easy for you to understand. I recommend you look at the ESV, Amplified, and NLT versions.

These translations are meant to be readable and full of extra help to break down the Scriptures you are reading and bring you more understanding of the text while they remain accurate to the original text. Next, I want you to find a Bible reading plan you can follow. BibleProject has amazing resources to start your Bible-reading journey. Next, fall in love with reading your Bible for understanding, relationship, and direction. Create a daily plan so you can be consistent with your Bible reading. It's the same way you improve your sport—by disciplining yourself to practice and improve every day.

Just as hydration is key to your physical fitness and health, so is prayer to your spiritual fitness and health. Take time to pray before you read your Bible. Ask God for understanding and for the Holy Spirit to be your guiding compass. But don't stop there! Get accustomed to praying throughout the day. It is amazing to communicate with your heavenly Father! You can bring anything up to him. Follow what God says in his Word, and incorporate his teachings into your life. If you have questions, research for answers and understanding, or ask a leader at your church or the chaplain on your team. If you do not have a church you attend, try to find one, or at least find one online where you can get sound biblical teaching. The next step is to find a small group that you can be part of so you can connect with other Christians to talk about life and the Bible. We all need accountability and community.

What we learn from our Bible reading, prayer, and time spent with God should ignite a fire within us to share the good news about who God is and what Jesus did for us on the cross with as many people as we can. Always remember, your actions make a statement. How you treat people, the decisions you make, and the way you carry yourself may be the biggest testimony for someone who is curious to know why you are the way you are. When they ask what makes you different from others, you can share with them that it's your relationship with God.

LET'S PRAY

Dear God,
I want to spend eternity with you one day. Please guide me daily

on how to live a Christian life that is pleasing to you. If I do wrong,
help me to repent for my sins and ask for the strength not to make
the same mistakes. Please also inspire me to share your good news
with others. Amen.

1. Find a Bible translation you will enjoy reading and understanding. Look at the English Standard Version (ESV), the Amplified Bible, and the New Living Translation (NLT) if you are a beginner. The ESV is often recommended for new believers because of its emphasis on word-for-word similarity to the original text in vernacular that is easy to understand. The Amplified Bible provides helpful study tools and seeks to bring clarity to the Scriptures. The NLT offers strong accuracy to the original text, is written in modern English, and is straightforward and easy to understand.
2. Pray for the Holy Spirit to lead and guide you daily.
3. Ask God to teach you what it means to be set apart while living in this world, but not of this world—and how to do that.

8 GOD IS EVER-PRESENT

God is our refuge and strength,
*   an ever-present help in trouble.*
PSALM 46:1

PREGAME

What do you see as the biggest ups and downs of competing in a sport? How do you respond to injuries, no playing time, or transition? When you're having a tough time in your sport, how do you respond to it?

My high school recruiting process was stressful at times—but it was also a fun experience. After attending different camps and taking my football and basketball visits, I ultimately chose to attend Miami University of Ohio to play football as a running back. During the recruiting process, Miami's assistant coaches called and visited my home. Then, ultimately, the head coach traveled to my house to visit me and my family, and I remember listening to him talk about his plans for me when I got to the school. That felt surreal. I thought that only happened in the movies. Once I took my official visit, experienced the red-carpet treatment, saw the campus, and visited with my best friend—who was a year older than me and already attending Miami—I knew I would commit to playing there.

Signing with Miami was one of the best moments of my life. It was a huge accomplishment, a major decision, and the culmination of a dream and goal I'd worked hard for. After high school graduation, I packed my bags and arrived on campus early that summer to get ahead of the curve, meet some of my teammates, build relationships, work out, and get in shape before the brutal two-a-days started. That summer was eye-opening. Immediately, I realized during the voluntary workouts that I was dealing with a high caliber and class of athletes. Everyone was faster, stronger, and seemed to be built different. These players were serious about their craft. This realization could have gone one of two ways: strike fear in me or spark my competitive side, motivating me to improve myself and keep up with my teammates. The plan was to step up to the challenge, work hard over the summer, and join the team in the fall as a respected freshman who kept his mouth shut and tried to outwork everyone else.

As time passed, I became more comfortable with the day-to-day summer schedule. One morning I walked down to the stadium and went to the practice turf to work on route-running with the quarterbacks. As I was running a route, I faked right, then left, and made a sharp cut to the right off my left leg. As I planted my foot in the turf, I felt an unusual stretch and heard a crunch that sounded like someone had crumpled plastic. When I rolled my ankle to the outside, I immediately knew I was injured.

This was incredibly upsetting to me. I felt like I had just found my rhythm with the team, and it was like the record had skipped a beat. I knew this injury was going to set my progress back, and I worried that my teammates would see me as weak. I also worried that I'd quickly get out of the excellent shape I'd worked so hard to get into. Fortunately, this injury only kept me out for a few weeks, and I was able to soon return to practice and workouts.

Besides getting injured that summer, I also received news that the coach who visited my home, gave me my scholarship, and announced all his plans for me was taking a head coaching position at another D1 school. I wondered what that would mean for my career. Who would be my head coach?

Things happen unexpectantly. Plans get derailed. But unexpected situations that change our path and direction aren't by accident. When times are bad and the seas of life are rough, we tend to get upset or blame God for allowing bad things to happen, and we feel like he is nowhere in sight. But that couldn't be further from the truth. Scripture says, *"God is our refuge and strength, an ever-present help in trouble."*

You better believe that God is there when you are upset, crying, angry, full of anxiety, depressed, lonely, and confused. He's also there for you when all is good. God is an ever-present help for you in the lowest of lows and the highest of the highs. We are imperfect humans living in an imperfect world with a perfect God who cares about our well-being. He is always present and right there when you need him.

=== **LET'S PRAY**

Dear God,
Help me to remember you love me dearly and are always there for me, both when I'm in a time of need and when things are going great. Thank you for being a secure, steady, and ever-present help in good times and bad. Amen.

1. Write down what you're dealing with right now—both good situations and bad situations—and talk to God about them.
2. It might be helpful to read about other athletes who have been through the highs and lows. I recommend *I Feel Like Going On* by Ray Lewis, *Quiet Strength* by Tony Dungy, *Who Am I After Sports?* by Darryll Stinson, and *Power, Money, & Sex* by Deion Sanders.
3. Take this week to thank God daily for who he is and tell him how grateful you are that he is ever-present in every area of your life.

PERSEVERANCE

But as for you, be strong and do not give up,
for your work will be rewarded.
2 CHRONICLES 15:7

PREGAME

Have you ever been in a situation that seemed unbearable or extremely hard to conquer? Do you ever feel like you don't have the strength to keep going? Do you sometimes feel like quitting?

GAME TIME

Despite loving sports and competition, I have felt like quitting plenty of times. Especially the very first time I played organized football at the age of six. When I told my dad I wanted to play football, he asked, "Are you sure?" Not thinking about why he was asking, I confidently—maybe too confidently—said, "Yes!" My dad was one of my football coaches, and I soon realized why he would ask me if I was sure I wanted to play the sport.

I'll never forget my first day of hitting in football pads. In the first tackling drill, we formed two lines—one of tacklers and one of ball carriers. The goal of the drill is for the ball carrier to run through the tackler and for the tackler to stop the ball carrier from running through them and scoring. I stood in the tackling line, and when I reached the front, my heart was beating so hard in my chest I heard it in my ears. I was nervous, anxious, and scared—all at the same time. Dad said, "Ready, set, go!" and the ball carrier ran toward me at full speed, dropped his shoulder upon my arrival, and left tire marks all over my chest. Well, at least that's what it felt like.

Without missing a beat, Dad told me to get up and go again. I looked at him and said, "Okay. Ready, set, go!" The next ball carrier ran toward me and completely trucked me. I lay there thinking, *Not again*, when I heard my dad's voice: "Get up and go again." I got up and reset. "Ready, set, go!" It happened again—I still couldn't tackle the next ball carrier. I felt myself getting angry as Dad told me to go again. This happened ten more times, and by then I was in full-blown tears, but I didn't want to give up. I knew that if I wanted to play the game, I needed to persevere through this seemingly impossible drill. I finally got so upset and hit the next guy with so much anger, passion, and tension while screaming that he fell flat on his back. I knew I'd just experienced my first real football tackle—and that is the moment I fell in love with the sport.

Football isn't the only area of my life where I've felt like I wanted to quit and give up. I know that if I didn't have a relationship with God, I wouldn't have been able to get through many of my trials—both in sports and in life. As I got older, I fell more and more in love with God and strengthened my relationship with him. I learned that this life is not about me or sports— those are just a small part of the big picture. I learned that life is about God using our gifts and talents to carry out his plan and about helping others.

We are to do our work as if it's for the Lord because it is. It's a given that you will encounter trials and tough times. The question is, how will you respond to those challenges? Will you quit, or will you persevere? God wants you to—and gives you the tools to—train with excellence, purpose, and passion. To learn from your mistakes. To take both your craft and your relationship with him seriously. To never take for granted the breath in your lungs or every opportunity you have to make a difference in the sports world, in the greater world, and in the kingdom of God. Don't give up, because your work for the Lord will be rewarded.

LET'S PRAY

Dear God,
Please help me to be strong and to rely on your strength when I'm
weak. When I want to give up and quit, please grace me with your
strength to persevere and push through. Amen.

POSTGAME KEYS

1. Your goal is to be unbending, sturdy, and immovable in your faith. Write down some things you can do that will help you achieve this goal.
2. Remember that your work, gifts, and skills are meant to be given to the Lord. When you feel like giving up or quitting, think about this truth.
3. Ask the Lord how you can incorporate him in every area of your life.

10 WATCH WHAT YOU SAY

Those who guard their lips preserve their lives,
but those who speak rashly will come to ruin.
PROVERBS 13:3

PREGAME

Do you enjoy talking trash with your competitors, teammates, or friends? Does the talk sometimes get heated? Have you hurt anyone's feelings with the things you've said? Have your feelings been hurt by what others have said?

I enjoy competition and the intensity it breeds. My dad taught me at a young age to keep my mouth shut and not trash talk my opponents. I did my best to follow those rules—until my opponents started trash talking me, and I felt compelled to finish it. Most of the time, I did my best to let my actions speak. However, there were times when things got intense, and I let myself get caught up in the moment. Thankfully, at those times God reminded me that I was going too far with my speech.

The words you speak matter. That's why it's so important to follow Proverbs 13:3 and watch what comes out of your mouth. There is much wisdom in guarding your lips, because you never know how a person may react to your unloving words. Someone could be having a bad day, and your harsh words could truly hurt them or cause them to react unkindly or even harm you. The wrong words could be a trigger for someone in a dark place and could cost you your career or your life. Unfortunately, this has been the case for many athletes, not to mention people on the streets in everyday situations.

Be aware of what you say and how you say it. If you gossip or tell secrets about others, there's a good chance your words will come back and ruin you. I'm not saying you can't have fun joking around with your friends, teammates, or coaches. I'm saying think before you speak. Be aware that your words hold weight. Your words impact both for the good and the bad. You don't want to say anything you will regret later because you didn't take the time to think before you spoke. God wants us to have acceptable, empowering, uplifting speech that edifies others.

You don't want to wait to incorporate this into your life. You can start now. Learning how to talk to your friends, teammates, siblings, parents, coaches, referees, and opponents will help you be successful in the long run. Leaders know how to uplift others and not bring them down. If you want to be a leader, a winner, a good teammate, and a role model for others, guard your lips and don't speak rashly—even if others are trash-talking you.

Dear God,
Please help me to watch what I say and how I say it. I don't want
to tear people down with my words; I want to build people up. Help
me to lead with words and actions that uplift everyone around me.
Amen.

1. Think before you speak. Constantly remind yourself of this, especially when someone talks trash to you or pushes you to respond in a negative manner.
2. Use your words to build people up rather than tear others down.
3. Pay attention to your surroundings. Do your friends influence you to speak differently from how God wants you to? If so, ask God to help you find better people to surround yourself with.

11

GIVE THANKS

. . . always giving thanks to God the Father for
everything, in the name of our Lord Jesus Christ.
EPHESIANS 5:20

Do you ever listen to athletes, celebrities, or other people in their interviews and hear them say, "I want to first thank my Lord and Savior Jesus Christ"? What do you think when you hear them speak those words? Have you ever genuinely thanked God for your accomplishments and all he has blessed you with?

The talents and giftings you possess are the things you naturally do exceptionally well. You may run extremely fast or have extraordinary quickness. Maybe you can jump higher than most, swim like a shark, or lift massive amounts of weight. You may be blessed with extremely flexible limbs, superior hand-eye coordination, or a brain that easily memorizes complicated plays. You might have been born with an insane amount of endurance and grit.

An abundance of these natural physical gifts can make you an excellent athlete, but it's important to remember that any of the gifts you possess were given to you by God. He created you to be the way you are, and he wants you to know your gifts and talents are connected to your purpose. I remember playing in a high school basketball game, having one of those special nights. It felt like the game was going my way in every way, but I knew my success was not solely from me. I knew God had given me the athleticism to do the things I did in that game to help my team win. So immediately after the buzzer went off, I said, "Thank you, Jesus. This could not have been done without you," in a private moment while walking off the court.

Then our local news and newspaper interviewed me. During my interview, I didn't start the conversation by thanking my Lord and Savior, Jesus Christ. I wasn't scared to talk about God in any way and thank him in an interview, but I didn't feel the need to force it into that particular conversation. The opportunity didn't come up, otherwise I surely would have, as I have in other interviews.

Paul tells us in Scripture to be connected and controlled by the Spirit. We should be consistently and constantly grateful and thankful for what God has done and is doing in our lives, and it's important to recognize that anything we do would not be possible if it weren't for God. I encourage you to thank God daily for breathing air into your lungs, waking you up each morning, giving you good health, providing you with an opportunity to make a difference in someone's life, and gifting you with your athletic ability. When the moment is right and you feel the Holy Spirit prompting you, look for opportunities to share how good God is with others.

Dear God,
I want to be used by you. I always want to be thankful to you. Help
me never lose sight of who you are in my life. Open my eyes to
opportunities when I need to thank and acknowledge you—both
publicly and privately. Amen.

POSTGAME KEYS

1. Practice giving thanks to God throughout the day, not just during church, at a Bible study, or at a certain moment like mealtime. Let giving thanks authentically be a part of who you are.
2. Tell someone close to you—a family member, a teammate, a coach, a mentor—three things you are thankful for.
3. Every day for one month, write down on a sticky note one thing you're thankful for and put it on the back of your bedroom door. At the end of those thirty days, see how many blessings God has given you. (And thank him for those blessings!)

12   SPIRITUAL ENDURANCE

Be joyful in hope, patient in affliction, faithful in prayer.
ROMANS 12:12

PREGAME

Are you spiritually equipped to endure challenging life situations, make difficult choices, and face adversity? How do you withstand the pressures of sports, life, expectations, and stress?

GAME TIME

Playing sports, besides being fun, is a great way to learn about teamwork, endurance, attention to detail, winning, losing, and just life in general. But it also can be demanding, stressful, tiring, traumatic, and the catalyst for off-the-field issues. It's a juggling act when athletes try to balance their sports schedule, schooling, friends, work, and a healthy spiritual life. When you feel overwhelmed, do you look to God for help, or do you tend to let the pressures of life overcome you?

We may be spiritually depleted if we find ourselves getting angry or irritable easily, or if we're operating with less grace for others. But there's a way to recharge our spiritual battery. When we *spend more time with God and learn about Jesus*, our love for the Lord increases. With increased love for Jesus, there is an increased love for people.

Romans 12:12 reminds us that we are equipped to have greater spiritual endurance by being joyful in hope, and the way we become joyful in hope is to believe in God's best for us because we know God is a good God who works all things for his glory and our good. There are things we can't control, and the sooner we realize that, the better off we will be as humans living in this world.

We can also dramatically build our spiritual endurance by carving out *time to pray daily*. You may start by scheduling a specific time to spend with God. However, let that evolve into continued prayer throughout the day.

Pray when you wake up.

Pray when you shower.

Pray on your way to school.

Pray on your way to the practice facility.

Pray before practice.

Pray before a game.

Pray during warm-ups.

Prayer is incredibly powerful for your spiritual endurance. When you are filled up with God's joy, it's easier to have patience in a heated, trying, or tough situation. You are less likely to operate and react from your flesh.

How do spending time with God and praying daily help us? They help us:

1. Be joyful in hope.
2. Be patient in affliction.

3. Continue to be faithful in prayer, by making it a habit and a lifestyle.

Typically, when you do well in your match, game, or competition—or better yet, you win the division, playoffs, sectional, weight class, or championship—you beam with joy. When you are filled up with time spent with God, you get a similar feeling, which helps you respond in a godly way to things that could derail you. Be joyful in hope, faithful in prayer, and strengthen your spiritual endurance.

LET'S PRAY

Dear God,
I need you daily. I can't be myself without my connection to you.
Help me to be more joyful, to have more patience, and to have a
desire to pray often so I can become spiritually strong. Amen.

POSTGAME KEYS

1. Romans 12:12 is a Scripture that you want to have hidden in your heart. It will give you hope in Christ and keep you spiritually fit. Memorize this Scripture this week. Place it on your phone wallpaper, laptop, or put it on your bathroom mirror, door, or wherever you will see it the most.
2. Choose how long you will pray each day this week. If you have yet to make regular prayer time a part of your life, start with five minutes daily and gradually increase it over the next few weeks.
3. Prayer is your superpower. Read Matthew 6:6, 9–13 which teaches you how to pray.

13   CHAMPION STATUS

Do you not know that in a race all the runners run, but only
one gets the prize? Run in such a way as to get the prize.
1 CORINTHIANS 9:24

Would you consider yourself competitive? Do you agree that only one competitor or team can get the prize? How much effort are you willing to put into winning that prize? Are you okay with second place, a participation ribbon, or just doing the bare minimum—or do you want to be on the winner's stand?

In today's Scripture, Paul compares living a life for Christ to competing in athletics. He wanted to give the early church a visual of what it looked like to live for God, and so he connected our faith to the Isthmian games, which were named after the Isthmus of Corinth. The Isthmian games were a festival that included competitions in music and athletics ranging from wrestling to chariot races to foot races and so many more.

In any type of competition, the top competitors and most successful athletes are not satisfied with a participation ribbon. These elite athletes work hard and strive to be the best at what they do. It takes a different level of commitment, consistency, and competitiveness to run in such a way to get the prize, win championships, bring home the gold, secure the number one trophy, and claim the top spot. If you're one of those athletes born with an extra shot of competitiveness, you can lead your teammates to win the race.

As Christians, we should approach our relationship with Christ in the same way. We shouldn't merely check items off a list of things Christians should do and give an average effort. We should apply that same gritty, hard-nosed effort to living a life of faith and receiving the prize. In fact, we should make even *more* of an effort. That's because the prize we are after as Christians is worth so much more than what we work so hard for in athletics.

If we compete with focus and determination in living life for Christ, we will win the ultimate prize in heaven: everlasting life with Jesus Christ. Just imagine hearing God say to you, "Well done, good and faithful servant.

Thank you for influencing your teammates and those who have watched you live for me. Thank you for competing with a higher purpose."

Work hard, have fun, learn, enjoy the process, give it your all, and play to win, but make sure God is at the center of all you do.

Dear God,
I humbly ask for the grace to be consistent in my efforts to live a
life that is pleasing to you as an athlete and as an ambassador of
who you are and what you represent. Help me to run the race well.
Amen.

=== POSTGAME KEYS

1. Take time to meditate on 1 Corinthians 9:24 and think of how it applies to your daily life.
2. Read the full chapter of 1 Corinthians 9 to get a bigger picture of what it means to run in such a way to get the prize.
3. Read the Bible and pray. The more you do these two things, the better your decision-making process and championship mindset become—both in athletics and in your Christian walk.

14 — REAL VALUE

For physical training is of some value, but godliness has value for all
things, holding promise for both the present life and the life to come.
1 TIMOTHY 4:8

=== PREGAME

Do you ever wonder how you can motivate yourself and your teammates to train at an optimum level consistently? Do you truly understand the

 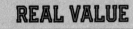

importance of what you do and how it impacts your performance? Is your training for both this life and beyond, or is it just about the here and now?

I don't think the average person understands the intensity of being an athlete. If you're a high-level competitor, you understand the long hours of training and the sacrifices made in your personal life—everything from your diet to your mindset to injury-prevention and recovery. Elite athletes strive to be the best, and their drive to succeed controls almost every aspect of their lives. They are meticulous with the details in each area of their lives and tenacious in their training and preparation.

I've had the privilege and honor to be both an athlete and a coach. I respected and appreciated most of my coaches but had less respect for others. The coaches I most respected knew who they were, knew their stuff, knew the game they taught, and knew what they represented. The very best coaches prepared their athletes for life outside of their sport. The athletes I looked up to and aspired to be were confident in who God said they were and didn't care if they caught splinters going against the grain. You knew without a doubt that God reigned supreme in their lives.

In 1 Timothy, Paul writes as Timothy's mentor, teaching him how to train for a life of godliness. Paul understood the need for physical training and that such training had value. The same is true for spiritual training. You must be trained well to live life for Christ. While physical training may be great for the present time, it holds zero weight for the eternal. To be trained well spiritually, you must appreciate how important overall godliness is for both now and the everlasting future. There are eternal ramifications to living a godly lifestyle.

Be an example for your teammates and others who watch you, inspire them to be elite, prepare them for life, and motivate them to be tenacious about living for God. You may be their only example of a Christian that could change the trajectory of their life.

Dear God,
Change me from the inside out. Spark a love for your word in me.
Please teach me how to live a godly lifestyle. I want to be an example
for other athletes, and I want to live a life of real value for you. Amen.

POSTGAME KEYS

1. Memorize 1 Timothy 4:8. Its words will set the tone of your approach to life.
2. Provide a safe and encouraging space for other Christian athletes to grow in their knowledge of God. How can you create an opportunity for your teammates to study the Bible together? Could you begin a prayer group within your team?
3. Ask God to lead you to be a witness to your team through your actions.

EXPECTATIONS

There is surely a future hope for you,
and your hope will not be cut off.
PROVERBS 23:18

PREGAME

What expectations are you dealing with right now? Are you expected to lead and inspire your teammates? What do you think you can do to meet your position or role expectations as an athlete?

GAME TIME

I once listened to a video clip of Deion "Coach Prime" Sanders answering a thought-provoking question: "What's the toughest thing you have encountered as a head coach?" He said, "Expectation—I can't expect out of them what I won't expect out of me." In our world, this statement rings true. How can you expect hard work, effort, consistency, follow-through, focus, and respect if you don't provide your coaches, teammates, and yourself with the same things? It can be a challenge to meet expectations—especially lofty ones. Because we are fallible human beings, sometimes we mess up, don't follow through, and do not meet expectations.

If you are a Christian, your coaches, parents, teachers, friends, and teammates should be able to trust your words and actions. And you should be able to trust God to help you meet the expectations he's set for you as a believer, such as that you are humble and willing to take constructive criticism, and that you treat others with fairness and kindness.

Ask yourself, *How can I represent Christ to those I come in contact with? How can my actions meet the expectations of my coaches or teammates so that I don't disappoint them and can show them the power of God?* Your goal is to meet and exceed their expectations, and the Creator himself will help you do it.

Let God's Word be your guide on how to live as a child of God and as an athlete who wants to be a light to your teammates and others in your community. Take the pressure off yourself. You don't have to be anyone else's savior. Still, you can be a bridge to the Savior by doing your part and meeting the expectations God has set for you.

LET'S PRAY

Dear God,
Please help me with any anxiety that I'm facing regarding expectations. Instruct me on how to meet my role's expectations while still enjoying the process. And help me to remember that meeting your expectations is the most important thing of all. Amen.

POSTGAME KEYS

1. If you're feeling the pressure of expectations, go on a walk, pray, and talk with God about what is heavy on your heart.

 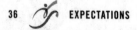

2. If there isn't a heavy burden on your heart, ask God to reveal what expectations he wants you to set for yourself, your teammates, and your community.

3. Find joy in the fact that there is an amazing future for you and know that God's Word is secure. Make sure your expectations of yourself line up with God's expectations of you.

16   BEHIND YOUR DOOR

The integrity of the upright guides them,
but the unfaithful are destroyed by their duplicity.
PROVERBS 11:3

PREGAME

Do you have a side of your personality that you show to your family or people at church and a different side you show to your friends or people online? Do you act differently behind closed doors when no one is watching you? If you answered yes, why do you think that's the case?

GAME TIME

When I was growing up, there was a guy in our neighborhood who was a great basketball player. When I saw him play, he reminded me of Penny Hardaway. His game was so silky smooth. He was older than me, and I just knew he was going to end up at a Division 1 college and then go on to play in the NBA. He was just that good. I looked up to him because he was a beast on the court, funny and friendly, all the ladies loved him, and he went to church. He was a modern-day superhero for us young bucks.

But I saw what he wanted us to see. What I didn't know was that he lived a double life. During the day and on Sundays, he was such a great guy, but behind the scenes he was a drug dealer. I was shocked as I watched the cops show up at his house to arrest him with guns drawn and their blue, red, and white lights swirling around the apartment complex. I knew then that despite his outward appearance, he hadn't been living a life of integrity. Sadly, it cost him his college scholarship and led to other problems he couldn't rebound from.

The word *integrity* in Proverbs 11:3 comes from the Hebrew root word *tummah*, which means "blameless, moral wholeness, without moral blemish." It doesn't mean that an individual who has integrity is perfect and without sin, but it does mean they try to live an upright and moral life. Whether people are watching or not, doing your best to follow God in every area of your life puts you on the right path and guides you to live an honest and fulfilling life. The only way to live that way is to have a healthy fear of God and desire to honor him with your actions. Only you know if you are honoring God with your life consistently—so are you?

While no one is perfect, pay attention to how you carry yourself in various social settings and ask yourself, *Is this who I am? Is this honoring God?* But don't stop there. To get a good indicator of who you truly are, monitor how you are when no one is watching. Is that person pleasing to God? If you're not, ask God to help you change from within so you can live an upright and godly life.

LET'S PRAY

God, I want my life to honor you both in public and behind closed doors. Please help me desire to lead a life of godliness and to authentically be the person you made me to be so I can proclaim you to the world. Amen.

POSTGAME KEYS

1. Write down these core words and hang them up where you can look at them daily: *integrity, honesty, respect, loyalty, faithfulness,* and *consistency.* Ask yourself, *Am I living a life in which I model these characteristics and honor God?*
2. Remind yourself that your teammates and coaches—along with

anyone you might have a brand deal with—can trust you if you have good character and integrity.

3. Choose a mentor or role model whose life shows integrity. Learn more about them and take inspiration from their life. How can you apply what you see in their life to your life? Reference Proverbs 10:9, a verse that is straightforward and easy to live by.

17 THIRST TRAPS

On reaching the place, he said to them, "Pray that you will not fall into temptation."
LUKE 22:40

PREGAME

Have you had to deal with temptation? How do you respond when you're tempted? What have you been tempted with that seems challenging to resist?

GAME TIME

We live in a world that saturates us with temptation. There is temptation to focus on ourselves and not on God. There is temptation to react to situations with anger and in a manner that is unpleasing to the Lord. There is temptation to cheat. There is temptation to partner with any brand that offers lots of money, even though that brand stands for things that may go against your convictions or morals. There is temptation from men and women at school, work, on your team, and on social media. There is temptation to lust after other people. There is temptation to want what others have. There is temptation to consume substances that are harmful to your body and your future.

None of us live free from temptation. Even Jesus was tempted.

Temptation isn't the problem, though. The problem comes when we fail to resist temptation and choose to indulge in it. That's when we sin. I would encourage you to read the entire twenty-second chapter of Luke. It describes a very intense time for Jesus, and God gives us clear direction for overcoming temptation. In Luke 22:40, Jesus tells his disciples to pray so they will not fall into temptation. Jesus was so serious about prayer that when he came back from his time alone in prayer and saw the disciples knocked out sleeping, he asked them, "Why are you sleeping? . . . Get up and pray so that you will not fall into temptation" (Luke 22:46). He repeated himself, and you know it's serious when Jesus repeats himself.

Imagine if you didn't work out, train hard, study your sport or play-book, eat right, take recovery seriously, or get sufficient rest. You would become weaker. This wisdom applies to your spiritual life as well. If you don't consistently pray, spend time with God, and read your Bible, you will become spiritually weak. When you are spiritually weak, it's harder for you to stay strong and say no to temptation. As an athlete, you are in the eye of the public, and a lot of people may find you cool, a commodity, or even a celebrity. Not everyone in your life has bad intentions. However, Satan always has bad intentions to ruin the image of God, and he will try to use anything or anybody to exploit your weaknesses.

Remember, God is always there to help you resist temptation and find a better path ahead.

LET'S PRAY

Dear God,
Thank you for being a loving Father who wants to preserve us
and keep us safe. Help me turn to you in times of temptation and
become spiritually strong so I can have an easier time saying no to
temptation. Amen.

POSTGAME KEYS

1. You are not strong enough to resist temptation on your own, but with God, you can overcome it.

 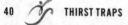

2. When you are tempted, call on God and pray a simple prayer asking him to help you not to be drawn in.

3. Temptations will always be there, but so will God. And he is all-powerful. Stay connected to the vine. Read John 15:5 to equip yourself to resist temptation.

HARD WORK PAYS OFF

All hard work brings a profit,
   but mere talk leads only to poverty.
PROVERBS 14:23

PREGAME

Are you the kind of person who talks a lot about what you will do? Do you share with everyone what your plans are? Do you finish tasks, or do you sometimes not quite make it to the finish line? Are you a hard worker, or do you have a lazy streak?

GAME TIME

It was a Friday night in Akron, Ohio, and I had just finished having my positional team meeting for our football game the following day against the Akron Zips. I headed back to my room with my roommate, who was also a running back, to unwind for the night and get some sleep. My roommate was dealing with an injury, but because he was technically the second-string running back, he was hopeful he could still play the next day. I was the third-string running back, and if he wasn't cleared to play, I would have an opportunity to make my college debut. I felt conflicted. I didn't want my roommate to be hurt because he was more than a team-mate—he was also one of my good friends off the field.

I had moved to Oxford, Ohio, right after high school graduation to do extra workouts, with the goal of playing at the collegiate level right away.

This was a moment I had focused on throughout my two-a-day training sessions and tough practices. I was continually reminding myself to work as though the Lord was there in the flesh as my coach, and I was determined not to disappoint him or myself.

The next morning, I woke up feeling refreshed and excited to hop on the bus to head to the stadium. My roommate was still in pain, though, and it didn't look like he could suit up for the game. That moved me up to the second-string position, and I knew the starting running back wasn't in great physical condition, so he would eventually need a break during the game. As the game got underway, my team was running the ball a lot and marching down the field against our opponents, and, as expected, the first-string running back started to look winded. The head coach looked down the sidelines and screamed, "Dooley! Get in!" Guys, I was so excited and nervous all at once. As I ran onto the field, I could only think about not messing up under those bright lights in front of my coaches, teammates, commentators, and parents in the stands.

While running onto the field, I tripped and fell. Just kidding. I just wanted to make sure you were paying attention. Actually, on my first drive I moved down the field with the team and scored my first touchdown. It was one of the best feelings I've ever had. I will never forget that moment. As I ran off the field and heard the cheers of my teammates and the fans, it felt good to know that I had seen and believed in this moment—scoring my first touchdown on my first drive after entering the game.

I love the book of Proverbs because it's full of wisdom and talks about hard work a lot. During two-a-days, I would read a proverb a day, and this Scripture especially stuck out to me: "All hard work brings a profit, but mere talk leads only to poverty" (Proverbs 14:23). I knew I didn't want to live a life of poverty. I also understood that when you're all talk and don't put in disciplined, consistent work, it can keep you from succeeding or finishing tasks.

It takes hard work to succeed as an athlete.

It takes hard work to be a student-athlete.

It takes hard work to juggle a schedule, including friends, family, and sports, and keep God first.

It takes hard work to follow through with your goals by finishing what you set out to accomplish.

Dear God,
I want to be a person who doesn't just talk about the things I plan
to do. I want to work hard and follow through and accomplish
things. Help me to understand that hard work pays off, and remind
me that when I work for you, I will always succeed. Amen.

POSTGAME KEYS

1. This week before you go to bed each night, write a task list for the following day. Write down everything you need to accomplish. Then, try to have everything checked off that list by the end of the evening.
2. Talk less about what you are going to do and commit to doing more.
3. Remember and reflect on this quote by high school basketball coach Tim Notke: "Hard work beats talent when talent doesn't work hard."

19 PURSUE RIGHTEOUSNESS

Whoever pursues righteousness and love
finds life, prosperity and honor.
PROVERBS 21:21

PREGAME

What are you pursuing right now? Success? A scholarship or a good school to attend? Making the team or becoming a starter or key contributor? Are you pursuing status over righteousness?

I knew a college basketball player who was skilled and loved the Lord. He was a walk-on, his work ethic and discipline earning him a spot on a championship team at a Division 1 school. It was a huge feat to accomplish, and he did not take it for granted. He got up at 4:00 a.m. so he could be the first one on the court, get some extra work in, and be warmed up and ready to practice with the rest of the team when everyone else got there. He juggled practices, games, training sessions, a full course load, a Bible study, and church.

He would have broken down if he hadn't pursued God throughout his college athletics journey. It's simply too hard to manage the stress of life without God at the center of it. As the apostle Peter urged, "Be alert and of sober mind. Your enemy the devil prowls around like a roaring lion looking for someone to devour" (1 Peter 5:8). Satan is always lurking nearby to kill, steal, and destroy. Satan will use traps, distractions, temptations, confusion, anger, loneliness, depression, stardom, pain, loss, and so many other methods to attempt to bring you down and tarnish your honor.

God wants you to pursue righteousness, a life of wisdom, a desire to live the way he wants you to live, and humble submission to him. The Hebrew word translated *pursue* in Proverbs 21:21 is *radaph*, which means "to chase, to be in great pursuit of, to run after." When we pursue righteousness in this manner, we will be successful in God's eyes.

We must constantly remind ourselves that sports are only a fraction of the big picture. Still, as athletes we have been given a unique opportunity to inspire others to desire to live a life of righteousness. Living a life of righteousness takes work. You may be made fun of, mocked, called names, or looked down upon. You may lose friends and be misunderstood because you live your life differently from others. However, if you stand firm and keep the faith, you will be a radiant beam of light in a dark world, no matter how much anyone tries to dim your light.

Pursuing everyday goals is awesome but look beyond the everyday and shoot for the eternal. Keep God at the center of your pursuits and pray that you will overcome challenges and adversity with grace and honor, acting different from the world, because you know God has your back.

Dear God,
I want to live a life of wisdom and pursue you and your righteous-
ness daily. You are such a good God who cares for all of us, and I
want to honor you with my life. Amen.

POSTGAME KEYS

1. When you commit to pursuing God as a way of life, he will guide
   you to wisdom and the peace of good choices.
2. This week, meditate on Proverbs 21:21 and ask God how you can be
   better at the practice of pursuing righteousness and love.
3. This Scripture is worth committing to memory! Write it on your
   game shoes, write it on your athletic tape, and etch it on your heart.

20   CHOOSE WISELY

Do not be misled: "Bad company corrupts good character."
1 CORINTHIANS 15:33

PREGAME

What type of friends do you have? Do the people you surround yourself
with make you a better person? Or do you feel like you could make wiser
decisions about the people you spend time with?

GAME TIME

When you go away to college for the first time, it can be challenging to
know how to handle your freedom. You want to enjoy your college experience, but you also need to learn some boundaries so you can actually
graduate and stay in college—and have a positive experience. That's why,
right from the start, it's imperative you choose your friends wisely. The
company you keep could directly impact your future—and that can either

work for you or against you. It's a breath of fresh air when you connect with like-minded people or meet people who are all on the same positive trajectory. But when you feel a check in your spirit, whether it's a hesitation to be around certain people or to go along with what your friends are doing, pay attention to that and recognize it's your spiritual Spidey sense going off—aka the Holy Spirit looking out for you.

A guy I know was in a situation in college where his roommates invited him out to do some crazy pranks but he didn't feel like he should go with them. They kept pressuring him to go out with them, but he felt in the pit of his stomach that he should stay back in the dorm and make it a gaming night. Plus, he had practice the next day. They made fun of him, but eventually they left him alone and headed out. Hours later, my friend received a call saying his roommate had been rushed to the hospital. The group had set fire to a couch that was in the bed of the truck they were driving. The roommate lost his footing when the truck accelerated, and he was launched off the truck and struck the back of his head on the side of the road when he landed. Unfortunately, the young man never recovered from the accident and passed away. The company he chose to keep was not a good influence on him, and it cost him his life. My friend was sad to lose his roommate, but he was also glad he made the choice to stay back in the dorms that night.

In the Bible, we learn that Paul heard about many problems going on in Corinth, so he wrote the church a letter about five areas that needed to be addressed: division, sexual misconduct, food, worship gatherings, and Jesus' resurrection. Our verse for today, 1 Corinthians 15:33, comes from this letter, which Paul wrote to help the Corinthian believers intentionally look at every area of their lives from the lens of the gospel. Believers were spending copious amounts of time with unbelievers and, over time, were being swayed away from their belief system.

You can spend some of your time with people who don't believe the same things you believe, but the problem occurs when you spend most of your time with people who hold different beliefs and standards. Time after time, we have seen this happen to many athletes. So, choose your circle wisely—guard your morals, be selective about the company you keep, and ask the Holy Spirit to guide you in your friendships.

Dear God,
Thank you for caring about my life. Help me to realize that who I
have in it will determine the path I take. Show me how to discern
who I should spend time with and who I should guard myself from.
Guide me in choosing my circle of friends wisely. Amen.

POSTGAME KEYS

1. Write out a list of your closest friends. Then, go through the list and ask yourself the following questions about each person: *Are they a good influence on me? Do they make me a better person? Do they make me want to be a better Christian? Do they hold me accountable for the things I do?* If not, reevaluate how much time you spend with those people, and ask God to bring better friends into your life.

2. One of my favorite Scriptures, and one I would suggest you meditate on, is Proverbs 13:20.

3. Memorize this Scripture: "The fear of the LORD is the beginning of knowledge, but fools despise wisdom and instruction" (Proverbs 1:7).

21 CULTURE FOLLOWS CHARACTER

Do not love the world or anything in the world. If anyone loves
the world, love for the Father is not in them. For everything in the
world—the lust of the flesh, the lust of the eyes, and the pride of life—
comes not from the Father but from the world. The world and its
desires pass away, but whoever does the will of God lives forever.
1 JOHN 2:15–17

How often do you think about being a success in today's world? Are there certain accolades or achievements you're chasing? Are your thoughts solely about you? What type of culture are you setting for yourself or your teammates?

Culture plays a big part in an individual's—and in a team's—success or failure. Did you know that culture follows character? If your coach or organization doesn't put up with individualism and wants every athlete to be a team player and a person of moral character, that is a recipe for greatness. That type of culture breeds good people who work hard, are willing to put the team first, and compete with grace. But if your organization, team, players, or coaches lack organization, discipline, and a moral code, that's a sure way to usher in toxic culture.

As an ambassador for Christ, a level of culture is already set for you. You are to treat everyone with love and respect, no matter if it's the coach, janitor, chef, president, or fan. You are also commanded to strive for and compete with excellence. In other words, you don't slack off. You train to outwork everyone else—not because you want the attention on you, but because you want to do your best for the Lord. It's all about whom you represent.

It's so easy to get caught up in what this world offers. It's both enticing and alluring. Satan is slick and will always find ways to poke at your weaknesses. It could be a desire for fame, finances, or the flesh. It could be giving in to the lust of the eyes or to pride. The world promotes those things as what we should desire, as if nothing about them is wrong and there are no boundaries or rules to how we should live. If Satan can confuse us and trick us into thinking the world's way is the best and God's way isn't worth it, he can eventually get us to perish along with the ever-decaying world we live in.

Instead, change your culture! Be a leader. Be the player, teammate, and friend that God has called you to be. How do you change the culture? By staying true to what you believe in. It's one thing to say you believe in Jesus—but then to act in a way that doesn't align with Jesus' character. By demonstrating kindness, compassion, and humility through your actions consistently, you can change the culture and solidify yourself as the leader your locker room can support.

There is so much greatness in you because of the God you serve. Dedicate your life to him, and he will lead you in all righteousness. And when this world ends, you will have lived a fulfilling, fruitful life and live in eternity forever.

LET'S PRAY

Dear God,
I want to live a life pleasing to your standards, and I want to be an
extension of you to others. Please help me be the catalyst to set the
culture you desire in my sport and on my team. Amen.

POSTGAME KEYS

1. You are not governed by the rules of this earth, which is led by Satan. You are led by the one true God in heaven.
2. In your prayer time this week, ask God how you can be a better leader as well as a better follower. They go hand in hand. It takes humility to do both well.
3. Here are a few character traits that make a good leader: humility, being quick to listen rather than to speak, self-awareness, respectfulness, empathy, being teachable, self-discipline, and having vision. Is this you? If not, work to be better in these areas, with God at the center of your life.

22 HUMILITY ON AND OFF THE FIELD

For all those who exalt themselves will be humbled, and
those who humble themselves will be exalted.
LUKE 14:11

What does humility mean to you? Think of someone you know who is humble—what stands out about their character and the way they live their life? Why do you think it's important to be humble?

Over the years, I have watched athletes from many different sports compete and communicate without humility. It's just not an attractive look. It can be easy to be cocky or arrogant, especially if we receive a lot of praise and accolades. All of us battle pride to some extent, but the goal should be to eradicate it. But without Jesus in our lives, it won't happen, no matter how nice you naturally are. And, unfortunately, exalting yourself is encouraged in this world.

My son just started playing flag football, and it's been such a blessing to watch him learn the game. The league that we are a part of has been great. They have implemented many rules to create an atmosphere for the kids to develop good character and sportsmanship. For example, after you pull off your opponent's flag, you hand it back to them. After the game is over—win, lose, or draw—you huddle up and give the other team a shout-out on three. These are the types of habits that help athletes learn foundational sportsmanship attributes. As we get older, if our coaches or organizations don't focus on good sportsmanship, we lose our ability to be humble because we are humans playing a competitive sport—and pride and arrogance can be contagious in those settings. The gladiator in you, mixed with high emotions and pride, can make you not want to shake your opponent's hand after a loss. However, that's if you rely on yourself instead of letting Jesus guide your decision-making. It takes humility to live a life pleasing to God as an athlete.

Humility starts with the heart. We all know many people who appear humble, yet it's false humility, and that type of humility reeks. Have you ever heard of the term "false hustle"? A player could dive after a ball after the play has ended to make themselves look like they are hustling, even though they weren't actually hustling during the play. That is false humility in action. However, we are built differently if Jesus runs our lives. The world expects us to be prideful and pompous, but as a follower of Jesus, we don't have to demand to be loved and seen, to seek a position of greatness, or to draw attention to ourselves. If you have faith that God has your back, you can just leave it in his hands.

God will elevate you in his timing, which is the right timing. All you have to do is work hard, trust God, be faithful, and be humble on and off the field. Allow God—not others—to elevate you, and don't worry about the rest. Be great in God's eyes, and you will be great.

LET'S PRAY

Dear God,
I don't want to be like the world thinks I should be—prideful, arrogant, self-centered, and existing to promote myself above others. I want to operate with humility and serve you and others with my life. Amen.

POSTGAME KEYS

1. Find ways to serve your teammates, coaches, fans, parents, siblings, and others through acts of kindness. Serving others will help you remember that we are all equal in God's eyes.
2. Surrender your pride to God and remember that your gifts and abilities come from him.
3. Make sure you pray daily. It keeps you close to God and reminds you how great God is and how blessed you are to live for him.

23 NO FEAR

Have I not commanded you? Be strong and courageous.
Do not be afraid; do not be discouraged, for the LORD
your God will be with you wherever you go.
JOSHUA 1:9

Have you ever felt nervous in a game, match, competition, practice, or when visiting a new organization or meeting a new coach? Were you ever scared of your competition? Have you faced hard times that felt like they would never end?

It's okay if you answered yes to some of the above questions. It's only natural that you occasionally feel a few butterflies in your stomach. It shows that you care and are serious about your sport. I've witnessed many teammates get nervous and throw up before taking the field. However, as soon as the game started, it was as if the nerves were turned off and beast mode was turned on. They turned into athletes with no fear.

My friend is a boxer who can shift gears like this. Outside of the ring, he is one of the nicest people I know, but inside the ring he's an absolute beast. One day we were in fight camp preparing for his upcoming fight. It was going to be televised, and he was feeling pressure to win and reclaim the belt in his division. All throughout camp, he worked extremely hard. There were moments I saw the pressure weighing on him because he knew it was not just about him; it was also about the people connected to him, those who would benefit from his victory.

To help calm his nerves, I sent him Joshua 1:9 to meditate on. These were the words God spoke to Joshua when he felt overwhelmed by the prospect of leading the children of Israel out of the wilderness and into the promised land. Joshua was fearful of leading a large group of people, fighting intense battles, and being the Israelites' spiritual leader. He knew he had to be strong, but he knew he didn't possess that kind of strength by himself—he needed to rely on the strength of God.

Like many of us in our own respective sports, Joshua was looked on to provide strength, leadership, and guidance. The pressure to do this could have overwhelmed him and filled him with fear, but the beautiful thing about Joshua—and about us today—was that his strength didn't have to come only from himself. God was his battery pack. And just like he received his power from the Lord, God is our source of strength as well. You need to learn all you can to be equipped to play and lead; however, you also need to apply your faith in God and trust that he will be your source of strength.

Look to God for guidance.

Look to God for peace that surpasses all understanding.

Look to God in your time of need.

Don't be discouraged; instead, be strong and courageous, because God is with you in every situation. You are a beast, and the one the enemy should fear.

LET'S PRAY

Dear God,
Help me to stay strong and courageous during tough times.
Remind me that you are always with me, and I can look to you
anytime I feel fearful or inadequate. Amen.

POSTGAME KEYS

1. Your source of strength doesn't come from your family, girlfriend, boyfriend, friends, coach, pastor, or yourself. Your strength comes from the Lord.

2. Memorize Joshua 1:9 this week. This Scripture is powerful and comes in handy when you're running on fumes.

3. Write out a list of things you fear in life and pray that God will have dominion over your fears. Once you are done praying, throw the list in the trash as a physical representation of you letting them go and giving your fears to God.

24 GET YOUR REST

Then God blessed the seventh day and made it holy, because on
it he rested from all the work of creating that he had done.
GENESIS 2:3

Would you consider yourself a night owl—i.e., do you like to stay up late at night? Do you feel like you function better as the day—and night—goes on? Do you get less than six to eight hours of sleep most nights?

We all take rest for granted until we are forced to prioritize it. Who doesn't enjoy staying up late occasionally to hang out with friends, play video games, travel, go to the movies or a concert, or have long talks? So many fun events take place late at night. I'm not saying those things are bad. However, when we work hard and exert our bodies, we are physically tearing ourselves down. Because of this, our bodies need time to rest, restore, and recover. If we don't find the discipline to make time for rest, our bodies will get our attention and force us to rest—often in the form of illness or injury. I know many athletes believe they are machines, but even machines break down from time to time.

The Bible tells us that God even made rest a priority, and he is God. He modeled taking a break so we would know to do the same. He knows we need downtime.

However, it's tough to get adequate rest when you feel pressure to be great at what you do and you have so many other things competing for your attention—you're going to class, studying hard, practicing for long hours, learning your playbook, spending time with friends, or maybe taking care of your family, being present for your kids, being a good spouse, and still having a social life. It's not easy. And it's extremely tough when you leave God out of it. God is our source of peace, and since the beginning of time, he has formulated an ancient pattern for us to abide by. He worked for six days and rested on the seventh day.

Without rest, you usher in health issues that directly impact your ability to perform. If you have poor sleep habits, you may develop daytime fatigue, reduced brain function, depression, anxiety, regression in memory, decreased muscle and injury recovery, and many more possible ailments.

Rest also has far more important rewards than just physical benefits. God wants to give you rest for your soul—a time when you can spend moments with him in prayer, meditation, and stillness during a Sabbath or scheduled rest time. This is a time for doing the relaxing things that bring you joy—reading, walking, playing video games, or going to your nearest coffee shop or chill spot. I also suggest setting aside time to unplug and turn off your phone. After you do this once or twice, you will realize how nice it is to be shut off from texts, calls, and notifications.

In addition, make sure you get enough sleep. Some of us need eight hours of sleep a night, while others need more or can get by with a bit less. When you sleep, your body has a chance to heal and reset for the next day. Try to establish regular sleep habits, including time to wind down each evening before bed. Then, when you wake up, give thanks to God each morning because he is the one who sustains you and keeps you going.

LET'S PRAY

Dear God,
Help me to appreciate and prioritize rest and not feel guilty about
taking time to relax and recover. Give me both spiritual and
physical rest so I can be all you want me to be. Amen.

POSTGAME KEYS

1. Plan out your week to allow yourself to get enough sleep. Schedule a bedtime and stick to it so you get six to eight hours (or more if you need it) of sleep a night.
2. Choose a day you will call your Sabbath and do not work. Make it a day of rest. You might start with four hours and, over time, add hours to it until you reach twenty-four hours.
3. The Hebrew word for *Sabbath* is *Shabbat*, which means "to stop." How often do you intentionally stop your actions, rest, and give time to God? This is an opportunity to align yourself with God and his natural rhythm. Pick the time of day you will start and the

time you will end your Sabbath. You can read a devotional from this book, pray, or meditate. As you close, you can listen to worship music, pray, or have a Sabbath meal. Find his rest for you.

DON'T RESPOND

Do not answer a fool according to his folly,
or you yourself will be just like him.
PROVERBS 26:4

PREGAME

How do you feel when someone attacks you verbally? Have you ever had someone leave hurtful messages on social media? How do you respond to people who try to provoke you?

GAME TIME

In 2016 I was blessed to win a competition that landed me the title of "Face of ReebokONE." It was an intense competition and process. However, it helped me learn a lot about myself, other people, social media, business ethics, and how to conduct myself in the public eye. There was one thing said to us Reebok athletes in a meeting one day that has stuck with me and has probably saved me from a lot of trouble, heartache, anxiety, and stress: "When you are an athlete or a public figure, so many people have so much to say about so many topics—whether others want to hear it or not. When people have something negative to say, you have one thing to do: *Don't respond.*"

This advice has been proven to be a game-changer for me. Social media trolls want someone to argue with. But if you don't respond, they can only leave a comment, and that's it—end of discussion. If that comment bothers you, it's your social media platform. You're in control. You can delete the comment and block their account. Sometimes someone catches you on the wrong day, and it may feel really good to respond to their negativity. However, don't take the bait. Instead, follow the wisdom given in Proverbs 26:4: "Do not answer a fool according to his folly, or you yourself will be just like him."

It's not worth getting entangled in a keyboard spat. I know, that sounds silly, right? But as soon as you respond to the foolishness, you've stooped to the level of the troller. Others watching from afar can't tell who the fool is and who isn't—both of you sound pretty ignorant. Proverbs 26:4 isn't just wisdom, it's also a safety mechanism to protect you. Trying to win social media arguments is just not worth it.

In your position as an athlete, you have so much good to offer to the world, and you may even have the ability to provide for your family, friends, teammates, and others. If Jesus was mocked, maliciously beaten until he was unrecognizable, spit on, and hung on a cross to die as an innocent man—and all that time never gave his trollers the satisfaction of responding in kind—you can do it in your provoking situations too. Let's learn from his actions and internalize this wisdom from the book of Proverbs.

LET'S PRAY

Dear God,
Help me to be able to pause when I see negativity coming my way.
Give me the grace to remember the words of Proverbs 26:4 and
apply your wisdom to my life immediately. Amen.

POSTGAME KEYS

1. You will be light-years ahead of your peers if you adopt the "Don't Respond" practice in your life.

2. The next time someone says something negative to you or tries to get under your skin, take a deep breath, walk away, swipe out of the app, and give yourself five minutes. Write your response back on a notepad or in the notes section in your phone to get it off of your chest, then erase it or throw it away.

3. Here are a couple of Scriptures to reference when you need to be reminded to withhold your response instead of reacting in the moment:

If a ruler's anger rises against you,
>   do not leave your post;
>   calmness can lay great offenses to rest. (Ecclesiastes 10:4)

But now you must also rid yourselves of all such things as these: anger, rage, malice, slander, and filthy language from your lips. (Colossians 3:8)

26   PICK YOUR HEAD UP

Why am I discouraged?
*   Why is my heart so sad?*
I will put my hope in God!
*   I will praise him again—*
*   my Savior and my God!*
PSALM 42:11 NLT

PREGAME

Do you ever feel overwhelmingly sad? Are you sad right now? Does it take you a while to recover from being discouraged? How do you cheer yourself up?

GAME TIME

Athletes tend to hide their feelings more than the general public, which can lead to unhealthy practices. Before I started writing this book, I spoke to more than a dozen athletes, asking them what issues and topics they would like to see in a sports devotional. Every one of them said, "Mental health issues and dealing with depression." That says a lot. According to the Gitnux Blog: "35% of elite athletes suffer from disordered eating, burnout, depression or anxiety, while only 10% of all college athletes with known mental health conditions seek care from a mental health professional."[1] This is alarming, and it is one more statistic that proves we need more attention and awareness of this topic.

A friend of mine attended a fitness conference where he heard a speaker insist that depression wasn't real. My friend said he became irate at the speaker's words, because he survived a deep depression battle that was extremely hard to overcome, and if it weren't for medical professionals and Jesus, he would not be alive today. Depression is a real thing, and it's something every athlete needs to be aware of. Every day, you deal with all kinds of pressure, high expectations, jam-packed schedules, and tough competition. You are scrutinized and picked apart by onlookers who sometimes forget athletes are also human beings. What you do isn't easy. Trying to juggle this lifestyle can weigh on you and put you at risk for depression and mental illness.

At the beginning of Psalm 42, the psalmist shares his hopelessness and frustration that God seems distant, even though he thirsts for him. We all share his sentiments at some point in our lives. But in verse 11, he shifts his tone to remind himself that although this time, season, or moment is tough, he will eventually have hope.

I may be sad, I may be discouraged, I may feel hopeless, but I will put my hope in God. I will praise him in the good and bad times, and I will continue to pursue and chase after him because I know God is faithful and he will not leave me. The enemy wants you to believe the opposite—to stay discouraged or depressed, isolating yourself from others and not getting help. *NOT TODAY, Satan!* The enemy will not win this battle.

If you're feeling the weight of discouragement and depression, don't be ashamed to ask for help regarding your mental health. Your God wants the best for you, and you can trust him with every aspect of your life. I believe in you and in the faithful God of the universe to deliver you and comfort you through your hard times.

---

1. Lorena Castillo, "Athlete Mental Health Statistics [Fresh Research]," October 31, 2023, https://gitnux.org/athlete-mental-health-statistics.

Dear God,
Thank you for being faithful to help me through the toughest times.
I will praise and honor you through all seasons of my life. Help me
not to be too proud to ask for the help I need. Give me the strength
and will to fight and pursue you daily. Amen.

POSTGAME KEYS

1. When you are depressed, chronically sad, or need help, please get in touch with a health professional or someone you trust, like your coach, teammate, pastor, small group leader, family, or friend.
2. You can fight depression in other ways too. Get better sleep. Change your friend group. Incorporate self-care into your routine, which could be getting a massage, taking time alone to read, spending time in nature, going to a coffee shop, drawing, hanging out with positive people, eating healthier foods, and adopting the Sabbath practice.
3. You need to make yourself a priority by making God a priority in your life.

27 FUNDAMENTALS

All Scripture is God-breathed and is useful for teaching, rebuking,
correcting and training in righteousness, so that the servant
of God may be thoroughly equipped for every good work.
2 TIMOTHY 3:16–17

PREGAME

Do you know the fundamentals of being a Christian? Has the Christian walk been confusing to you? If you feel yourself slipping away from walking with God, how can you start fresh and live a Christian life as God wants you to?

Nowadays, there are so many ways to learn about anything. Information on just about any topic is at your fingertips, and there are now so many gurus in every field that it can be confusing to know if they are sharing correct information or just giving you their point of view. When it comes to learning about Christianity and God, there are some fundamental details we need to understand so we have a strong foundation to stand on.

Christians believe there is only one God and he is the Alpha and Omega, the beginning and the end. God is one God who eternally exists in three distinct persons—the Father, the Son, and the Holy Spirit. This is a major part of the foundation of Christianity, which is the doctrine of the Trinity.

Matthew 1:23 tells us about the birth of Jesus: "'The virgin will conceive and give birth to a son, and they will call him Immanuel' (which means 'God with us')." Christianity is centered around the life, death, and resurrection of Jesus Christ. When you read the Bible, you will learn fundamental truths about the life of Jesus Christ. You'll discover how God sent Jesus, who was God in the form of man, to come down to earth and teach us and give us a chance at eternal life. You'll find out all about Jesus being crucified on a cross, dying for our sins, being resurrected after three days, and then ascending into heaven, with witnesses watching it happen.

Christians also believe Jesus will return to earth in an event called the second coming. Again, the Bible tells us more about this: "But about that day or hour no one knows, not even the angels in heaven, nor the Son, but only the Father" (Matthew 24:36). Christians believe the Bible is the true, inspired written word of God, meaning it's reliable and originated from God, not man. There's a lot to learn, but we must take the time to read the Bible for ourselves if we want to discover more about who God is.

It's one thing to read the Bible; it's another thing to understand the fundamentals of it enough to apply it to your life. BibleProject has great resources to equip people to learn about God and his Word. I encourage you to check them out so you can learn the basic process of reading the

Bible in a fun, aesthetically pleasing, in-depth way.[2] The Bible is a beautiful body of work with a message that transcends generations and applies both to our current day as well as our eternal destiny.

When you read the Bible, remind yourself that you are reading the words of the living God. These are alive, transformative words that will continually shape and impact your life. Think of the Bible as your fundamental training guide. It equips you for life. It convicts you when you are heading in the wrong direction or doing wrong. It helps you get on and stay on the right path. It is the key to living life as God wants you to live it.

LET'S PRAY

Dear God,
Please help me internalize the foundations of Christian living and
not be confused by the ideas of the world. Help me to realize that
the Bible is my training ground for life and guide me to your truths.
Amen.

POSTGAME KEYS

1. Here are some of the fundamentals to remember. There is only one God, and he is the Alpha and Omega, the beginning and the end. God is one God who eternally exists in three distinct persons—the Father, the Son, and the Holy Spirit. Jesus was born to a virgin, crucified on a cross, died for our sins, resurrected after three days, and ascended into heaven. Christians believe that Jesus will return to earth in the second coming.

2. The Bible is inspired by God. It is God-breathed. Remember this because people will try and discredit your beliefs and the Bible.

3. Here is a powerful Scripture I want you to memorize because this is the foundation of your spiritual life.

---

2. This page is a good place to start if you're interested in using BibleProject for your Bible reading: https://bibleproject.com/explore/how-to-read-the-bible/.

Therefore everyone who hears these words of mine and puts them into practice is like a wise man who built his house on the rock. (Matthew 7:24)

 KNOCKIN' ON HEAVEN'S DOOR

These are the words of him who is holy and true, who holds the key of David. What he opens no one can shut, and what he shuts no one can open. I know your deeds. See, I have placed before you an open door that no one can shut. I know that you have little strength, yet you have kept my word and have not denied my name.
REVELATION 3:7–8

═══════════════════════════════════ PREGAME

Have you ever gotten upset when an opportunity didn't work out? What do you do when your plans fail? Do you trust God to help you make the right decision when you're offered an opportunity?

═══════════════════════════════════ GAME TIME

After I graduated from college, I bought a one-way ticket to San Diego, California, because I knew God was calling me to the West Coast. I wasn't sure why. I just knew that was where he wanted me to go. I'd known this since my sophomore year of college when I went with one of my teammates to Los Angeles during spring break. We stayed with his uncle, and after that trip, I knew I would end up somewhere in California. The feeling didn't change through the rest of college, and while working on my senior thesis I kept seeing California everywhere I looked. I fell in love with a show called *The O.C.* because of the aesthetics and topography of Newport Beach.

Based on my visit to L.A. and *The O.C.*, I often fantasized about living in Southern California, and then one day I took a break from writing my thesis and turned on the Discovery Channel, which was airing a whole episode about San Diego. My mouth dropped open as I imagined what my life would look like there. Later that week, I received a call from a college friend who had graduated a year before me, and I was surprised to find out she ended up in San Diego. Immediately, I asked her a million questions about what living there was like, what church she was attending, how expensive it was to live out there, what she was doing for work, and everything else you could imagine. When we ended the call, I dropped to my knees and said, "God, if you don't want me to move to San Diego, please shut the door of this possibility. I do not want to be out of your will for my life."

Later that month, that same friend called me and told me she had seen an ad at her church seeking a Christian roommate for a group of guys. I immediately called the number listed in the ad, spoke to the guys, and told them I knew God was calling me to move to San Diego. Long story short, after asking me some questions and having an easygoing conversation, the guys offered me the room. Mind you, I didn't have a job lined up yet, or even transportation for when I got there, but God gave me confidence in the process, and I had crazy, outlandish faith that it would work out because it was God's leading. It all happened so fast, and God did not shut any doors. In fact, he did the opposite and flung open all of the doors.

You may be wondering if the school you're considering is the right school for you, the team you want to play for is the right team for you, or the sport you want to play is the sport you are supposed to play. And, most of all, you may wonder if God is leading your situation. Instead of spending too much time worrying about everything, ask God to show you his will. And know that he is faithful. Revelation 3:7–8 was part of a letter to the church in Philadelphia, which took their relationship with God seriously. They knew Jesus had the key to open and shut doors, which would guide them to advance the gospel. Put your situation in God's hands. Instead of stressing about it, trust that he will open or shut the doors to opportunity and that he always does what is best for you.

Dear God,
I want to have more faith in you and trust that you have my best
interest at heart in every area of my life. Close the doors that need
to be closed and open the doors you want me to walk through.
Open my eyes to see your perfect plan. Amen.

POSTGAME KEYS

1. You can't go wrong when you give your opportunities to God. His closed doors are a blessing because they lead you to an open door elsewhere.
2. When you try to force a situation to happen or an opportunity to come to pass without including God in it, you are putting yourself above God. That is a dangerous place to be. Let God lead you.
3. Reference these Scriptures to remind you that God is in control. And if it doesn't go as you planned it, do not get discouraged. It's for the best in God's good plan.

> Then Jesus told his disciples a parable to show them that they should always pray and not give up. (Luke 18:1)

> This is the confidence we have in approaching God: that if we ask anything according to his will, he hears us. And if we know that he hears us—whatever we ask—we know that we have what we asked of him. (1 John 5:14–15)

29   IMPERFECTLY PERFECT

For all have sinned and fall short of the glory of God.
ROMANS 3:23

Do you ever feel like you must be perfect for your family, friends, teammates, coaches, social media, or church? Do you believe that perfection is a destination you can reach?

We live in a world where perfection is the end goal. Many of us work tirelessly to have the perfect game, perfect match, perfect fight, perfect race, or perfect score. The media adds to this, putting us in competition with others in the same field or sport, comparing our athletic prowess to the next person. I have had so many conversations with friends and other sports enthusiasts on who is the GOAT (Greatest of All Time): Michael Jordan or LeBron James? Is it because it's entertaining to argue or prove a point? And is this a healthy thing to do?

Unfortunately, I see pressure to be perfect happening in the one place we should feel safe: the church. People look to Christians as a model for a higher standard. They walk into church, and they're disappointed because it does not feel any different from the world they are accustomed to. I've heard so many people talk about encountering Christians who act as if they have never sinned in their lives. These Christians treat new believers, or those recommitting their lives to Christ, as less than, which makes it hard for non-Christians to feel accepted by the church, much less give their lives to Christ.

Christians who try to appear perfect are actually turning away people who need Jesus. When you represent God, do it in love. You don't need to lower your standards; however, you can't forget that Jesus died on the cross for your sins and imperfections. You were never perfect, and you will never be perfect. There is only one perfect person, and that is Jesus Christ. Paul made this clear in Romans 3:23 when he said, "All have sinned." He didn't mean some. He means every last one, without any exceptions. There are no tiers to how bad you sin—sin is sin, and we all fall short. That's why we all need a Savior.

Don't let anyone make you feel less than because of your past or your mistakes. At the same time, remember that being a Christian athlete does not make you better than the next man or woman you encounter. Be thankful that through the death and resurrection of Jesus, we have become perfect in God's eyes. Our goal is to be obedient to God and repent for the sins we commit every day. Hold your fellow believers to a high standard, but judging them or nonbelievers is not your place, because we all have fallen short of the glory of God. Only Jesus is perfect. If we believe in him, we can accept our imperfections as we do our best to follow the example of his perfect life.

LET'S PRAY

Dear God,
Please help me not to act "holier than thou" or see myself as better
than someone else. Help me to embrace the idea of being imperfectly
perfect and to live with humility and treat others with love. Amen.

POSTGAME KEYS

1. This week, memorize Romans 3:23 for your protection. When your heart feels judgmental, recite this Scripture to yourself.
2. We all have a past and want to be delivered and forgiven for our sins. Treat others as you would want to be treated by God.
3. This week, read Matthew 7:1–5. This will give you a great perspective on life and how you should treat others. It will help you have more grace for those around you.

LIGHT IT UP

You are the light of the world—like a city on a hilltop that cannot
be hidden. No one lights a lamp and then puts it under a basket.
Instead, a lamp is placed on a stand, where it gives light to everyone
in the house. In the same way, let your good deeds shine out for
all to see, so that everyone will praise your heavenly Father.
MATTHEW 5:14–16 NLT

What does it mean to be the light of the world? Do you know anyone you would call a light in our world? Do you think you are a light for others?

It's incredible to go out into the wilderness at night, where there aren't any streetlights, and look up at the sky and the stars. It reminds us how powerful light truly is. It doesn't matter where you are. Light cuts through the darkness.

We need light in our individual lives, just like our world needs light. There is so much darkness we read about in the news, see in school, look at on social media, experience on our sports teams, and witness in our communities. Everywhere we look, others need our light. To be light, we must reflect, reveal, and respect the source of our light. Ephesians 2:10 says, "For we are God's masterpiece. He has created us anew in Christ Jesus, so we can do the good things he planned for us long ago" (NLT).

We are here on this planet to do more than impress others with our athleticism, charisma, and popularity. We exist to advance God's kingdom on earth. As Christians, we are supposed to be the light of the world, to reflect who Jesus is. The world is "in the dark" about God, but as representatives of Christ, we "turn on the lights." Light allows people to see. We allow the world to see how much God loves them and what Jesus has done to restore their relationship with him.

If we are to be the world's light, we should carry out the same purpose Jesus had in coming to earth.

You can be a visible representation of Jesus. The goal is not that people will say, "Wow, those Christians are awesome. Look at all the amazing things they do to help people." Rather, the goal is that people will say, "What a great God they follow." The only way that will happen is if we make it clear that we are living moral lives and doing good deeds because we follow Jesus. If we don't give God credit, we are not being a light to the world. If we do good but fail to point people to Jesus, we haven't done what light should do. Being "light" means people can see that God is the source, purpose, and cause of any goodness in our lives.

Dear God,
Thank you for being light and shining through us so we can be
used to draw more people to your kingdom. Use me to pierce the
darkness and point others to you. Amen.

POSTGAME KEYS

1. To be light, we must reflect, reveal, and respect the source of our light—God.
2. When you are a light, you show others how good God is. Think of some action steps to take this week that will shine the light of God on the people in your world—and make sure the glory points back to the Lord.
3. I challenge you to be friendly to everyone you encounter this week. Smile more often and give them your full attention. When you do, you will be shining the light as you show them the love of the Lord.

31   JESUS IS ENOUGH

And my God will meet all your needs according
to the riches of his glory in Christ Jesus.
PHILIPPIANS 4:19

PREGAME

Do you ever wish that you had more—more stuff, more fame, more success? Have you ever looked back and realized God blessed you with the very things you wished for, yet you still didn't feel satisfied? Why do the things of this world seem more important than Jesus at times?

I love connecting with middle school, high school, and college-age youth. I've worked in youth ministry, which is so much fun, and I have also had the privilege of coaching high school football. Those times were priceless, and I wouldn't be shocked if I do it again one day. I loved having a small group of athletes I met with weekly to study the Bible, eat pizza, munch on snacks, and watch a show. We also sometimes cracked open Madden NFL and competed against each other. Those genuine moments of community centered on the life and love of Jesus were life-altering both for the students and for me. There were times we had upwards of forty guys packed into a room, sharing their hearts in a vulnerable way. It was amazing, and sometimes heartbreaking, to hear their stories about the issues they were dealing with and how the Lord helped them through.

An atheist joined our group solely for the community aspect, because he didn't have anyone else to hang out with. We knew he was an atheist, but we still treated him with love and respect and welcomed him with open arms. After a couple months of meeting with us, he pulled me aside after a Bible study and told me he wanted to give his life to Christ. He said he was only an atheist because his girlfriend was, and when they broke up, he couldn't deny the fact that he felt Jesus was real. Our group hadn't done anything extra special other than operate and treat people as Jesus shows us how to treat them in the Bible, because we believed that Jesus was enough. There is nothing wrong with being creative with your approach to sharing the gospel, but the message of Jesus is strong enough to stand on its own.

If your true mission and purpose is to bring God glory, you will be a blessing to others. As a bonus, because God gets the glory, you will be blessed abundantly. You don't need to use worldly gimmicks or lower your standards to "reach a demographic of people." Jesus is enough and always will be enough.

Dear God,

Please help me not to be tempted to be like the world. I always
want to remember that Jesus is enough, so help me not to worry
about adding anything else. Amen.

POSTGAME KEYS

1. Memorize Philippians 4:19 to combat the idea that you need to do more or be more to fit in with the world and share Jesus with others.
2. Don't overcomplicate Jesus. He alone is enough. Read Ephesians 3:20, 1 Peter 5:7, and Luke 1:35.
3. Remember, with God in your corner, you lack nothing.

NOT WORTH IT

Be alert and of sober mind. Your enemy the devil prowls
around like a roaring lion looking for someone to devour.
1 PETER 5:8

PREGAME

How often are you offered a drink, drugs, or substances you know are harmful to your body or mind? Is it hard to say no to your friends or social settings? How much pressure do you feel to do things you don't feel comfortable doing?

GAME TIME

I was made fun of in high school because I chose not to drink alcohol at parties. I rarely went to parties, but when I did, they had ginger ale or Hawaiian Punch there for me. It wasn't always that way. It took time for others to have respect for me and eventually leave me alone in that department. They tried to pressure me to party like they did, but I was too competitive and determined—there's no way anyone would guilt me into getting drunk or high. Was it easy to endure the ridicule? No. However, I knew it wasn't worth jeopardizing my future by losing control of myself and being altered by a substance. Those moments are what the devil salivates for. He can influence you to do things you wouldn't normally do when you are not in your right mind. I know some athletes who consume or smoke before practice or a game. Eventually, though, it catches up to them.

When you're feeling pressure to do what everyone else is doing, look to God's Word. First Peter 5:8 warns us that the devil is prowling around like a roaring lion, looking for its prey and trying to stop us from progressing the kingdom of God. That is why it's important to be sober-minded and alert. You will celebrate victories, win championships, attend parties, and have fun enjoying life. However, always keep this Scripture in mind so you don't put yourself or others in harm's way.

And I mean *always*. I was so good about not drinking or using, but I could have ruined my future in college because of a breakup and the choice I made following it. Instead of dropping to my knees and crying out to God in prayer or reaching out to some of my Christian teammates, I gave in to the pressure of the world. I was so sad, mad, and angry that—literally fifteen minutes after my breakup—I smoked weed from a bong for the first time and wandered around campus late at night, out of my mind. That was the lion lurking around, waiting for that one moment of vulnerability. Thankfully, I didn't do anything crazy that could have ruined my life. When I got home and was back in my right mind, I knew I would never do it again.

Unfortunately, I've heard countless stories of others doing something similar yet choosing to make bad decisions. As a result, they lost the scholarship, lost friends, or worse. And all for what? One moment. One experience. One night. When you're put in that position, ask yourself, *Is this worth it?* Then ask God to give you the strength to say no and be a light to others. You have way too much to lose and nothing to gain by giving in to temptation. Stay alert. You can fight better that way.

Dear God,
Help me say no when I'm tempted to consume alcohol, drugs, or
other substances that could alter my state of mind. I want to be
used by you, and I don't want to set a bad example for others who
look up to me and know that I follow you. Amen.

POSTGAME KEYS

1. One of your keys to making clear and concise decisions comes from being sober-minded. Remember this whenever you're tempted to make bad decisions.
2. Always ask yourself, *Is this worth it?* when you're asked, encouraged, or pressured to participate in drinking or doing drugs.
3. Set up parameters and stay disciplined. Accountability in our Christian lives helps us grow closer to God and be more like him. When we are weak, we need help, accountability, support, and strength from others. Make sure you set up those positive relationships in your life.

33 ELITE FOCUS

For the Spirit God gave us does not make us timid,
but gives us power, love and self-discipline.
2 TIMOTHY 1:7

PREGAME

Do you ever feel like you need more focus in order to accomplish certain tasks? Do you tend to procrastinate on projects or things that need to get done? What distracts you from being focused?

I don't know about you, but I love and appreciate the off-season. This is when you get to rest up and honestly critique your technique, execution, and overall game and put together a plan to get better for the next season. I know that watching and hearing about how you can improve is not always fun, but if you want to be great you need to learn to have thick skin and an eye for detail so you can eliminate mistakes and improve your skill set. Every athlete in every sport can always find a way to be better, and the off-season is the best time for those with an elite focus to work on it. You can consult coaches, mentors, or trainers, but ultimately, you are the one who needs to harness the strength, focus, and discipline to train and work on your goals, day in and day out.

In the Bible, Timothy also needed encouragement and guidance in a couple areas in his life where he needed to grow. He struggled with a spirit of fear and was a bit timid—maybe due to his particular personality and the lack of a positive male role model in his life. Paul wrote to him to give him encouragement and specific instruction about how to handle certain struggles in his ministry for the Lord and how to do better in the future.

Paul's words helped Timothy, and they can help us too. Paul endured much pain, loneliness, suffering, assault, and abandonment so he knows what it's like to encounter distractions, hard times, and unexpected hardship. Yet do not have a spirit of fear or lose your focus and discipline.

Setting big goals and striving to reach them is hard. Doing God's work is hard. To be the best at your sport and to have a great relationship with God—to be elite—you must learn to fall in love with discipline, marry consistency, elude distractions, run from procrastination, handle adversity gracefully, and plug yourself into the main power source . . . God.

LET'S PRAY

Dear God,
Help me not to have a spirit of fear or a lack of focus, but to stay
connected to you daily. You are my source of strength, discipline,
and focus. Amen.

1. If you have trouble achieving big goals, try creating a focus chart. First, write down your big goals. Then, underneath those, write down a few smaller, more bite-sized goals that you can work toward in order to achieve that big goal.

2. Make sure you celebrate each small goal as you complete it! This will help you feel successful along the way, which will make it more likely you'll stay on track toward completing your bigger goal.

3. Here is a Scripture to help you maintain elite focus when you're tempted to get distracted: "Let your eyes look straight ahead; fix your gaze directly before you" (Proverbs 4:25).

FREAK ACCIDENT

And we know that in all things God works for the good of those who love him, who have been called according to his purpose. For those God foreknew he also predestined to be conformed to the image of his Son, that he might be the firstborn among many brothers and sisters.
ROMANS 8:28–29

PREGAME

Have you ever been involved in a freak accident? How do you respond to an unplanned injury? Do you have people you can talk to when unexpected things occur?

GAME TIME

At the time of writing this particular devotion, I was laid up in bed with compression wraps around both legs, icing them, and wincing now and then because of the pain I felt in my hamstrings. Two days prior, I had a freak accident that should not have happened. I was playing outside with the neighborhood kids, getting a particular kid back for throwing water on me. (I'd specifically asked them not to get me wet because I was holding my satchel, which had my Kindle in it.)

After I got wet, I teased the kids and told them I would get back at them individually. As I was sneaking up on one of them, just as I was launching the bowl with water in it, I lost my footing, and my left leg slid out in front of me. I hyperextended my left knee and strained my right hamstring as I tried to get both feet back on the ground. But instead of landing upright, I ended up falling—hard. As pain shot up my legs and intense cramping began, I immediately knew it was bad. I didn't panic, but I was mad at myself. I had to go to urgent care, where they told me I'd need to have physical therapy. All that because of a water fight with the neighbor kids!

After the incident, I thought a lot about what happened. I searched my heart and asked God what I needed to learn from the situation. It wasn't a woe-is-me moment, though I did feel sorry for myself. Rather, I knew there was something to learn from the situation that would ultimately shape and mold me to be more like Christ. In my search for God's lesson, I came across Romans 8:28–29.

Most people look at Romans 8:28–29 and get excited about verse 28 and trail off at 29. If you are actively trying to be more like Christ in how you live your life, it's true that "in all things God works for the good of those who love him, who have been called according to his purpose," *as it says in verse 28*. However, if you do not love God and continually work to be "conformed to the image of his Son," as it says in verse 29, you can't expect verse 28 to ring true. Verse 29 makes sure we mirror the behavior and character of Jesus. In all things God works for the good of those who conform to God's image, not those who conform to the world.

How you conduct yourself, speak, and treat people says a lot about how much you love God. If you are mean, evil, ugly, and treat people with disdain, that's not the fruit of God in your life. And Paul writes, "In all things God works for the good of those *who love him*" (emphasis added). When an unexpected or freak accident happens, take a deep breath and ask God what you can learn from it. Those moments can make you stronger and be a blessing in disguise, growing you to more deeply appreciate life, loved ones, and current opportunities.

LET'S PRAY

Dear God,

I want to learn to love you more and follow you better. Please help me learn how to handle the unexpected situations that happen in my life. Help me to see things the way you do and to deal with adversity the way you want me to. Amen.

POSTGAME KEYS

1. Write down or talk about a few unexpected moments that have happened in your life. Take time to ask God, "What is this event's significance? How can going through it make me more like you?"

2. When you encounter adversity, start by taking a deep breath and counting to three. Then, ask God to help you stay positive and remove the negative thoughts by replacing them with, "God, I thank you that I have an opportunity to be more like you," and think before you react.

3. Use these Scriptures to help you during times of adversity.

   We are hard pressed on every side, but not crushed;
   perplexed, but not in despair; persecuted, but not abandoned;
   struck down, but not destroyed. (2 Corinthians 4:8–9)

   And the God of all grace, who called you to his eternal glory in
   Christ, after you have suffered a little while, will himself restore
   you and make you strong, firm and steadfast. (1 Peter 5:10)

35

*Whatever your hand finds to do, do it with all your might, for
in the realm of the dead, where you are going, there is neither
working nor planning nor knowledge nor wisdom.*
ECCLESIASTES 9:10

PREGAME

Do you ever need help following through on the things you need to do? Do
you have lofty goals and start strong but tend not to finish them? Have you
wondered why that is?

GAME TIME

The great thing about sports is that they teach you a lot about life, responsibility, teamwork, ownership of your actions, and adversity, as well as
about yourself. You have a purpose. You are not here by accident, no matter what anyone says. You are not here to aimlessly trot through life. As a
Christian, you have so much to do as a representative of Christ. As an athlete, you have a large stage on which to make an impact. Whatever sport
you play, whatever skill you learn, whatever job you take, whatever project
you work on, you should do it to the best of your ability and appreciate the
opportunity you have rather than simply check off a task on a to-do list.
Not everyone gets these same kinds of opportunities.

You get to step into that ring and fight.

You get to run onto that court and compete.

You get to run onto that field and clash.

You get to walk onto that clay court and battle.

You get to run onto that track and race.

You get to dive into that water and contend.

You get to step up to the plate and swing.

You get to enter that gymnasium and perform.

You get to bring glory to God with your work ethic.

There will be a day when you will need to focus your energy on something other than competing in sports. For today, try to exceed what is expected of you, and don't play down to the level of your competition or surroundings. When you change your mindset from simply wanting to achieve goals for the sake of achieving goals to achieving goals so you can give God glory, you won't want to fall short of following through. Be the one who sets the temperature at practice, in the classroom, in team meetings, in competition, and in how you approach life. Work hard with humility and honor. Strive to do it all well.

LET'S PRAY

Dear God,
I want to be a finisher. I don't want to fall short of my goals and misrepresent you. Please help me be diligent and unafraid of practice and hard work. Help me to do everything well. Amen.

POSTGAME KEYS

1. Remember, you represent God in all you do. This should change your mindset and work ethic.

2. List a few things you might be able to improve on (for example, working harder in the classroom, putting more effort into learning your plays, having a better work ethic during the off-season, making wiser decisions outside of school).

3. Give thanks to God for gifting you with special talents. Keep figuring out ways to remove distractions that keep you from excelling and try to have a short memory when it comes to your mistakes. Don't dwell on them and let them set you back. Learn from them and move on.

36   BLESSINGS AND BURDENS

Walk with the wise and become wise,
*   for a companion of fools suffers harm.*
PROVERBS 13:20

Therefore, as God's chosen people, holy and dearly loved, clothe
yourselves with compassion, kindness, humility, gentleness and patience.
COLOSSIANS 3:12

PREGAME

When people think of you, do they see you as a blessing? Do you display the love of God to people who give you bad customer service? How do you treat your teammates—with love, or are you selective? Are you good at including all your teammates and friends, or are your relationships exclusive? How can you ensure that your treatment of others will be seen as a blessing?

GAME TIME

One night as I prayed over my kids and family, I felt the Lord wanted me to pray that the Dooley family would be a blessing to others and not a burden. When my kids show up to school I want the teachers, staff, and their peers to see the Dooleys as a blessing rather than as a burden. I wanted my son at the tender age of six to display a great attitude on the flag football field and to his teammates. I want Dooleys to be known as team players, confident but not cocky, well-mannered, and humble.

As Christian athletes, this is how we should conduct ourselves. We are representatives of Christ, so our actions and presence should bless others both on and off the field. It is God's heart and desire that his followers treat everyone with love and kindness. Is it easier said than done? Absolutely.

That's why we need Jesus. That's why we need to spend time with him, intentionally working toward learning more about who he is.

God desires that we put on love, kindness, compassion, humility, patience, and a gentle spirit every day. When these are our attributes, we are a blessing to others. If we return to our old ways—before Christ—and treat others with malice, ill intent, a bad attitude, rudeness, unkindness, and are unloving, we become a burden to others. We become a burden to our teammates, teams, schools, families, and communities, and we discredit our opportunities to share the love of Christ with others. That's also how you lose friendships, job opportunities, connections, NIL deals, brand deals, and other opportunities.

Don't strangle your blessings and block your opportunities to be a blessing. My prayer for you is that wherever you go, people will see you as a blessing and a light.

LET'S PRAY

Dear God,
I want to be a blessing and not a burden to others. I want to be
cloaked in compassion, love, kindness, humility, gentleness, and
patience. Help me to be aware of my actions and attitude and
accurately represent who you are on a daily basis. Amen.

POSTGAME KEYS

1. You are only human, which means you will make mistakes. But let it be the desire of your heart to repent and work toward blessing others. Meditate on this Scripture: Ephesians 4:29.
2. Strive to be a blessing everywhere you go. Read Proverbs 11:25 this week to inspire you to be generous with your life.
3. People pay attention to how you treat others. As a Christian athlete, you are in a position to impact so many people positively. Grab hold of those opportunities.

JEALOUSY

For where you have envy and selfish ambition, there
you find disorder and every evil practice.
JAMES 3:16

Have you dealt with jealousy from your friends, teammates, or siblings? How does it make you feel? What about you? Are you low-key jealous of anyone because of their athletic success, their good relationship with a coach, their social media following, or how they are treated by the media and fans?

GAME TIME

When I was injured in high school and had surgery on my knee, I experienced complications from the anti-inflammatory medicine that was administered to me. The local news covered my recovery, and I got word that many teammates—guys I'd gone to war with on the gridiron—were upset because the news was covering me instead of them. These guys had a few choice words to say about me while I was laid up in the hospital, trying to will myself back to health so I could return to the field with my team. Hearing what they said about me—especially as I fought so hard to get back into playing form—didn't feel good. I felt B.A.D., as in betrayed, anxious, and demonized. I became a recluse, reserved and resentful, until God got a hold of my heart and reminded me that while it was evil for them to act that way toward me, it was equally evil to feel the way I felt. God convicted me of the desire for revenge that brewed in my heart. To combat those emotions, I wrote poetry, prayed, and placed my faith in God, counting down the days until I could get back on the field and play ball.

Jealousy is rooted in selfishness, insecurity, fear, resentment, and anger. And, as you heard in my story, your mental health can be negatively affected if you're a victim of jealousy or if you harbor any of those feelings in your own heart. It doesn't feel good when you encounter jealous individuals who project their insecurities on you, and being jealous of others doesn't feel good either. But because we are human, we all have experienced envy in some way.

You may be dealing with people who are jealous of you, or you may be feeling jealousy toward someone else. If so, do yourself a favor. Let it go. Operate from a place of purity, positivity, and peace, and watch how those blessings from God will overflow into other areas of your life.

LET'S PRAY

Dear God,
Please remove any hint of jealousy, envy, or insecurity within me.
When I encounter jealousy directed at me from others, please help
me to be strong and not be affected by it. Amen.

POSTGAME KEYS

1. Don't let evil defeat you and take you out of your game; instead, choose to defeat evil with good.
2. Protect your mental health by praying that God will help you remove any signs of jealousy, envy, insecurity, or anger toward others.
3. Focus on God and not the drama. "I keep my eyes always on the LORD. With him at my right hand, I will not be shaken" (Psalm 16:8).

38   TRUST THE PROCESS

Until the time came to fulfill his dreams,
the LORD tested Joseph's character.
PSALM 105:19 NLT

Are you impatient at times? If you could make all your dreams come true right now, would you do it? If so, why? If not, why not?

Joseph in the Bible was given dreams about his future that had not yet come to pass because he wasn't ready. He had to undergo a process to prepare him for his purpose. If he had bypassed the necessary steps to walk into his destiny, he might not have been mature enough or equipped for the challenges of his calling. Joseph had to go through a refining process. And, honestly, most of us are in that same boat.

We may want to start now.

We may want to play varsity right away.

We may want to get drafted in the first round.

We may want to be the star player immediately.

We may want a certain NIL deal.

We may want to be the team captain right now.

But thank God it's not you right now. It's not you, because it's not your time yet. Everything is beautiful in God's timing—not your timing. Don't force a position or platform your character can't keep you in. Unfortunately, that has happened far too often to amazing athletes who didn't have the patience to trust the process and become seasoned, so they could properly withstand the position given to them. There is a maturation process that needs to take place. Use your times of waiting to learn about who God is and develop spiritual habits that will provide strength, wisdom, and protection as you mature. Trust in God's process.

All of us walk a different road to get where God intends for us to go. Some may include heartache, trying times, and disappointments while others include incredible opportunities and successes. Each one will shape and mold you into who God wants you to be.

We can all be impatient at times. It's a normal human condition, which is why we need this reminder to trust God and his process. God doesn't make mistakes, and he isn't about to start making mistakes with you and your process. Find comfort in the grind. Delight in learning more about God. It will impact your view of him and illuminate his power in your life. Trust God, and trust the process.

LET'S PRAY

Dear God,
Help me find joy in the process and the journey you have me on.
Help me to trust you when I'm headed to the next level, and also
help me to trust you when I need to wait. Amen.

POSTGAME KEYS

1. Ask yourself, *How do I see God?* Do you see him as your dictator, provider, comforter, father, or punisher? Focus on seeing God positively if you currently have a negative view of him. Look at what Moses went through and was able to accomplish only because of God's provision. Read his story in Exodus, Numbers, and Deuteronomy.

2. If what you desire to happen hasn't happened yet, it doesn't mean that it won't happen at all. It means that God isn't ready for it to happen—and that when the timing is right, the right thing will happen.

3. Write out some of your dreams and save them in the notes section on your phone or stash a written list in a safe place. After some time has passed, look back at that list of dreams and see if they came to pass or if God surprised you with something far greater than you imagined.

---

39   A GREAT DAY TO BE GREAT

This is the day the LORD has made.
   We will rejoice and be glad in it.
PSALM 118:24 NLT

Have you ever woken up on the wrong side of the bed and chosen negativity for the day? What most often affects your mood, and how can you change it?

We all have had days where we would rather choose violence than peace. Well, maybe not to that extreme, but for some reason, we don't feel like smiling, greeting, hugging, or being pleasant to anyone. If you ever feel that way, know that today is your day. You are reading this devotional today for a reason. Today is a great day to be great!

Your mood is your decision. It is completely your choice if you want to be negative, upset, and angry. But today is the day the Lord has made, and I encourage you to choose to rejoice in it! There is a purpose for you today. Lift your chin, hold your head high, look at yourself in the mirror, and thank God for your existence and for that dog in you. It's time for you to practice having a great outlook on life.

If you are in a bad mood at this point in the devotional, that should have changed by now. If not, stop feeling sorry for yourself. Shake it off and show the world your will to be great.

If you have to attend class or go to work today, know that God allowed you to learn and impact someone else's day through your actions. If you have practice today, set the tone through your hard work, positive attitude, grit, and gratefulness for another opportunity to improve. Be excited if you have a game, match, meet, competition, or fight today. This is your chance to execute what you have been working on, and this is your opportunity to give God the glory. If you get to give back to the community today, be elated. Someone before you laid the foundation and was selfless to provide you with the opportunity to give back.

This is a great day. So, go out, rejoice in the Lord, and be great!

Dear God,
Help me to be aware of how blessed I am to wake up each morning

to a day filled with opportunities. Please help me to make a positive effort to be thankful and carry out the purpose and plan of my life. Amen.

1. You have to be intentional about being grateful, thankful, and positive.
2. Think of a variety of ways you can make today—and every day—great. Start by spending time with the Lord.
3. Create a positive daily morning routine. You might include these: wake up, pray, brush your teeth, shower, make tea or coffee, listen to worship music, read your Bible, do a devotional, and eat breakfast.

40 ONE STEP AT A TIME

So do not fear, for I am with you;
do not be dismayed, for I am your God.
I will strengthen you and help you;
I will uphold you with my righteous right hand.
ISAIAH 41:10

PREGAME

Are you currently recovering from an illness or injury? How are you dealing with the in-between time? How do you handle the recovery period when you are impatient to be healed already?

GAME TIME

It's not easy to be in a holding phase, waiting to recover so you can return to doing what you love to do. Your mind becomes idle, your thoughts become louder, and fear sometimes fights for space. During these times, it can be hard not to let doubt creep into your thoughts and drive you crazy. I want you to know that God is with you throughout the recovery process and will never leave your side. It's important to know that by his strength, not by your own strength, you will overcome.

If you are injured, fellow athletes may empathize with you, but some may not. It's not that they don't care; they just haven't had to deal with the level of pain you're experiencing—or the length and grind of the recovery process. However, I know someone who does get it. Not only does he understand, but he will always be there with a shoulder to cry on, his supernatural arms spread wide open to wrap you in his loving arms. God wants to walk with you through the process. He will even put the right people in your life and the right messages in front of you to bring you encouragement and peace during your trying times.

Let God hold you up and help you through your recovery one day at a time. Follow protocol from the medical professionals who are there to help you recover quickly. Reflect on what you are gaining out of the situation and take it into the next season of your life when you are fully mended and ready to get back out there.

LET'S PRAY

Dear God,
I need you and your strength daily to carry me through the best
and the toughest seasons. I know you are always with me, and I
ask you to give me strength when I'm weak. Amen.

POSTGAME KEYS

1. Read Isaiah 41:10 daily to remind yourself that you are not alone in your fight and that God will give you the strength to overcome.
2. Who can you talk to when you feel discouraged? Write those names down and save them in your favorites list in case you need to reach out to someone during your lowest points.
3. Read Romans 8:37 to give you the strength to overcome.

41

In their hearts humans plan their course,
  but the LORD establishes their steps.
PROVERBS 16:9

How do you respond when plans change? Are you a go-with-the-flow type of person, or does it bother you when things don't go the way you thought they would?

She had it all figured out. After high school, she planned to take her talents to a Division 1 college to play basketball on a full-ride scholarship. After college, she planned on getting drafted into the WNBA and having a long career in the pros, representing God and bringing glory to him as a Christian athlete. When she first set out to accomplish these goals, she trusted that the Lord would help her see them through. But ultimately, he had other plans for her life. She did play Division 1 basketball on a full-ride scholarship, and she had an incredible college career, broke several records, and set the school record for the most three-pointers made in a single season.

Her WNBA career, however, didn't go as planned. She played for four seasons in total, but her career was marred by injury. After she tore her ACL, she rehabbed hard to get back into playing shape. She was able to return and grab a spot on a roster but was cut right after the first pre-season game. That was it for her WNBA career, and she was left trying to figure out the rest of her life.

Sometimes your plans don't go the way you imagined them. There is nothing wrong with making plans for your life; you just need to be flexible enough to know that you should listen if God wants you to take a different route. In the Bible, you can read about all of the plans Paul made for himself, and you can also read about how God intervened and changed the course of those plans. God will direct your path as well.

God wrote your book of life already. He knows your beginning, your in-between, and your end. He has your best interests at heart, and even though your plans may seem better to you right now, I guarantee you God will outdo you. His path may be different, but if you trust him, his way always exceeds your expectations.

Countless times I've looked back and thought, *Wow, thank you, God, for leading me in a different direction. My plans were so minuscule in comparison to your plans for my life.* God knows your heart, and he can help you reach the destination or attain the desire you long for. Stay connected to him, be sensitive to the Holy Spirit's nudging, and follow his path for your life—even when it's hard.

LET'S PRAY

Dear God,
You are always so good to me. Thank you for caring so much about my plans, goals, and overall well-being. Please help me to be sensitive to your voice, to always run my plans by you, and to follow your direction. Amen.

POSTGAME KEYS

1. Proverbs 16:9 is one of my favorite Scriptures of all time. I've watched it save me from so much heartache, and God never failed to exceed my expectations. I challenge you to commit this Scripture to memory, so it is always tucked away in your memory bank.

2. Knowing that God is always in control is such a beautiful thing. Read Deuteronomy 31:8. This will give you confidence when you feel discouraged.

3. Recognize what you can control and what you can't control. Immediately let go of what you can't control and let God handle it. Then develop a motto for yourself that will help remind you God is

ultimately in control. Place this in your locker, phone, or wherever you can see it when you need a reminder.

BE YOURSELF

Therefore, I urge you, brothers and sisters, in view of God's mercy, to offer your bodies as a living sacrifice, holy and pleasing to God—this is your true and proper worship.
ROMANS 12:1

PREGAME

Do you sometimes wish you could have someone else's life or personality, and so you attempt to imitate it? Rather than trying to be like someone else, have you thought about what it might mean for you to offer your body—all your gifts and talents—to the Lord as a living sacrifice, as a child of God who is created in his image?

GAME TIME

Hollywood does a great job of glamorizing violence, drug abuse, and negativity. The media love to create a tough guy/girl persona that appears attractive and strong and is associated with boss-like qualities, boatloads of money, bold jewelry, lavish lifestyles, and bigger-than-life personalities. But that's not necessarily the life God desires for us.

If you are playing on a team or competing in an individual sport and have a chance to do something with your life, don't throw it away by trying to be something or someone you are not. Too many amazing athletes have the opportunity of a lifetime to play the sport they love at a high level, but then they throw it away by not staying true to who they are.

The choice is yours. You can embrace the personality, the behavior, the lifestyle that God has gifted you with, or you can embody a different personality, mode of behavior, or lifestyle that comes from another athlete.

Remember, you have the one thing they may be searching for—God. They may be trying to fill a God-sized hole with fame, money, sex, drugs, alcohol, friends, you name it. But you already have God, and with God in charge of your life, you are safe and secure, and you can find joy and purpose in living your life as God created you to live it.

You don't have to be someone you're not. You don't have to attend every party or keep up a certain reputation. You just have to offer yourself to God as a living sacrifice. You just have to live your life for him.

And as you do, be assured that God will fight for you and will elevate you to the level you need to be (whether high or low) to give you the influence for his kingdom that he wants you to have.

The apostle Paul's wisdom—a wisdom spoken long ago into the lives of God's holy people in Rome—applies to your life right now. When you offer yourself as a living sacrifice and decide to no longer conform to the patterns and values of today's culture, you are equipped to thrive in your endeavors. Embracing your identity in Christ and your giftedness, which is unique to you, will position you for finding contentment and purpose.

It's not worth gaining whatever the world has to offer—your scholarship, draft capital, playing time, starting position, money, sponsorships, and so much more—only to give in to being someone or something you aren't. Let who you are on the inside—your true identity—come to expression as you offer yourself as a living sacrifice to the one you follow as Lord of your life.

LET'S PRAY

Dear God,
Give me the confidence to be true to who you created me to be.
Surround me with people who encourage me to be my authentic
self. Help me discern the right influences to have in my life. Amen.

POSTGAME KEYS

1. The choice is yours. If you want to live a godly life and be used by God, keep him at the center, be yourself, and let God use the

authentic you. You can play a huge part in changing the trajectory of someone's life.

2. Write down this Bible verse and tack it up in a place you will see it every day: "Thank you for making me so wonderfully complex! Your workmanship is marvelous—how well I know it" (Psalm 139:14 NLT). Read it in several different translations, and you will be blessed to know that you are intricately and wonderfully made.

3. Don't worry about being influential. God will elevate you in his timing and in the way he sees fit. Take comfort in knowing that, no matter what, everything is in God's control.

43   GAME DAY

And whatever you do, whether in word or deed, do it all in the name of the Lord Jesus, giving thanks to God the Father through him.
COLOSSIANS 3:17

PREGAME

What do you do on game or competition day? Do you have a routine you go through to get ready? How do you get your mind right so you can go into battle focused?

GAME TIME

I want to help you bulletproof your nerves and give you the secret sauce to step into any match, competition, battle, or game ready to ball out. Most of the time, we think about so many things before game time—who we are playing or competing against, our own stats or times, what we need to do to win, the crowd, the venue, outside pressures, family in the stands, our coaches, our teammates, scouts in the audience, etc. I could keep going, yet none of those things will settle you down the way one simple but very important thing will.

During my freshman year in high school, I was getting ready to start my first varsity basketball game. I had practiced and played against tougher competition in AAU basketball that summer, but I was feeling a lot of pressure for this high school game, since I was a freshman starting over a senior in front of a huge crowd, playing on a team with high expectations to win that season. I always want to do well and be great, but I hate messing up and losing game than I love winning. In pregame, I reviewed the plays, the scouting report on the other team, and the guy I would be guarding, who happened to be the best player on their team. Because of my athleticism, I was matched up with him to try and stop or slow down his scoring.

While shooting in pregame, I envisioned myself playing stellar defense, making moves on offense, and putting the ball through the orange cylinder. I could even hear the sound of the ball swishing through the white nylon net. Although I thought this visualization was loosening me up, I must have looked uncomfortable, because my dad walked onto the court and asked me to come over to him. I jogged over with the ball on my hip, and he asked me how I felt. "I feel good, Dad. I'm ready to ball out tonight." Then he said something that immediately slowed everything down and lifted all the stress off of me: "Remember why you get to do this and how you got put in this position. It's because of the Lord—he put you here. Relax, and do this unto the Lord. Take yourself out of it, have fun, know your assignments, and bring God the glory. Thank him for this opportunity, your gifts and talents, and pray before you step back onto the court."

Thank you, Dad. I still do those things every opportunity I get—in sports and in life—and we would all do well if we followed his advice. Always remember who you do this for, who gave you the gifts and talents you possess, and who put you in the position you're in right now. Knowing this will bring you peace and allow God to use you.

LET'S PRAY

Dear God,
Thank you for putting me in this position with an opportunity to
bring you glory with the gifts and talents you have given me. Help

me to play loose, inspired, intelligent, and to the best of my abilities, and also help me to have fun. Amen.

1. Pray alone with God before every game, match, or competition. Use the prayer above and modify it as you get more comfortable praying.
2. Be thankful for God, be thankful for the gifts and talents he has given you, and be thankful you get to do what you do in sports.
3. Here are a few ways to calm your nerves before a competition.

   ▶ Take slow, deep breaths.
   ▶ Close your eyes and visualize yourself calming down and performing your sport well.
   ▶ Create a pregame playlist that will calm you and help you focus on God, peace, and succeeding in your competition.

44   KEEP PUSHING

But as for you, be strong and do not give up,
for your work will be rewarded.
2 CHRONICLES 15:7

PREGAME

How do you feel when you fail at something? Does it make you want to work harder or give up?

GAME TIME

Stop saying you can't. The sooner you stop saying you can't do something, the sooner you will realize you can do more than you think. You need to remind yourself who your source of strength is.

I know it's tough to see someone else in a similar race but farther along. Don't give up. Keep pushing.

I know you feel like you are working as hard as possible, yet no one sees you. Keep pushing.

I know you are making plays, yet nobody is patting you on the back. Keep pushing.

I know you are getting up earlier, staying up later, and not getting recognized for it. Keep pushing.

I know you feel as if you still need to prove yourself. You don't. Keep pushing.

I know you feel like you deserve a fair chance. It's not your time yet. Keep pushing.

I know you feel like you are running out of time. You're not. Keep pushing.

If you are struggling with waiting, patience, and timing, and you feel discouraged or even angry, you may want to shift your focus off yourself and your situation and focus on Jesus. Second Chronicles 15:7 is a great reminder for when we have these feelings and want to throw in the towel and quit. Don't give up. Keep pushing. Trust God. It's already out of your control. Stop trying to change the narrative and rewrite the script. That's too much work for you to try to undertake. God sees you giving your all. He's paying attention, and he is in the blessing and rewarding business. Galatians 6:9 says, "Let us not become weary in doing good, for at the proper time we will reap a harvest if we do not give up."

When facing tough times or hard situations, don't try to shoulder it alone. Ask God for guidance and wisdom through prayer and conversations with him throughout the day. Ask God to send mentors, pastors, friends, or leaders into your life who will talk to you about your frustrations and walk you through the hardships you are dealing with. Let him help you.

===================================== **LET'S PRAY**

Dear God,
Please give me the strength to keep pushing. I don't want to be

*someone who gives up at the first sign of resistance. I want to keep
fighting and discover all you have for me. Amen.*

1. Don't be quick to quit when you feel resistance. Trust me. You don't
   want everything to be easy. The process of getting to your goals
   builds character and strength.
2. Reflect on what you have quit in the past and why. Read
   2 Chronicles 15:7 again, and remember this verse the next time
   you feel like quitting.
3. If you want to quit something right now, write down what it is,
   share it with God, and ask him to help you through your situation.

45   WHAT'S NEXT?

*For our light and momentary troubles are achieving for us
an eternal glory that far outweighs them all. So we fix our
eyes not on what is seen, but on what is unseen, since what
is seen is temporary, but what is unseen is eternal.*
2 CORINTHIANS 4:17–18

PREGAME

Are you someone who tends to worry about the future instead of enjoying
the present? Do you think about what's next? Are you in a rush to get out
of your current situation?

GAME TIME

One of my daughters can sit at the table and finish having lunch, and
before she puts the dishes in the sink, she will ask my wife, "What are we
having for dinner?" We like to tell her, "We just ate; let your food at least
settle first and appreciate the meal you just had." The way our world is

nowadays, we are conditioned to never be satisfied. There is always something better out there. We must have the latest and greatest shoes, clothes, tech, cars, headphones, smartphones, or homes. How often are we upset that we do not have something? Maybe you feel less than because you don't have what your teammates have, whether it's materialistic things, physical attributes, or status.

I love progressive thinkers. I appreciate those who think about what's ahead, but I want to challenge you to think about what's ahead here on earth and also what is ahead eternally. Imagine some of the decisions we might make if we don't take the time to think about our eternal ramifications. In 2 Corinthians 4:17–18, God didn't say the Christian life would be easy. However, the Scriptures are clear that although it may not be easy, it is well worth it. We can easily focus on what we can see right now: the pain in the news, in our lives, in the losses of friends or family members, in our sports defeats, and on social media. All these things can keep us from focusing on what we can't see.

We play a large part in what God is trying to accomplish through us here on earth. Sometimes, life flat-out hurts, and it seems too daunting, discouraging, and disheartening to be a Christian. Just know that the pain you experience mentally, physically, and spiritually pales in comparison to the impact you are making for the glory of God through your obedience and faith. I want to encourage you and remind you to fix your eyes on the unseen, not the seen, because the seen is temporary and the unseen is eternal. Life goes by fast; seasons of life fly by quickly. Don't find yourself so entangled in the weeds of life here on earth that you're prevented from seeing the majestic blooming of what's to come.

=== **LET'S PRAY**

Dear God,
It's not always easy for me to see life the way you do. When I'm wondering what's next, help me to fix my eyes more on the unseen and less on the things I see daily. Amen.

1. What are you focused on right now? Write down everything that comes to mind: the good, the bad, the in-between. When you're done, pray over the list and ask God to remove the weight of the unknown off your shoulders, then meditate for ten minutes on how good God is.

2. Write down how you felt after you took ten minutes to meditate. Calm? At peace? Closer to God? Remember that feeling throughout your day.

3. I want to give you these Scriptures to remind you to take one day at a time.

> Therefore do not worry about tomorrow, for tomorrow will worry about itself. Each day has enough trouble of its own. (Matthew 6:34)

> Can any one of you by worrying add a single hour to your life? (Matthew 6:27)

46

HD X GIS (HEAD DOWN X GRIND IN SILENCE)

Those who guard their mouths and their tongues
keep themselves from calamity.
PROVERBS 21:23

PREGAME

Do you feel the need to tell people about yourself and what you plan on doing, or would you rather say nothing at all? Does staying silent benefit you or hurt you? If you choose yes, is it because you are excited and you want to share your enthusiasm with others? Do you want them to be impressed with you and your goals and aspirations?

Sometimes it feels great to share your excitement about your plans. You feel passionate about your goals and your future, and you want everyone around you to know it. Bear in mind, though, that oversharing isn't always the best route, especially if your follow-through game isn't great—in which case it can be hard for people to trust your word. At the same time, if people don't understand your passions or can't see the destination like you can, they may discourage you from accomplishing your task by poking holes in your dreams, goals, or plans. Try the "Head Down X Grind in Silence" approach—stay silent and work hard on your aspirations, keeping your plans to yourself for the time being.

William Shakespeare said, "Have more than you show; speak less than you know." The Bible also gives us good advice about our speech, our tongue, and what we should and should not say. If we aren't careful, our tongue can bring a lot of grief, trouble, pain, and problems into our lives. That's why it's wise to guard your mouth, hold your aspirations close to your chest, and walk out your plans rather than talk about them.

When I was in high school, I told my friends, parents, and brother that I would get a full-ride scholarship to a Division 1 school in football or basketball, and I was determined and worked hard to make that dream a reality. However, my proclamation didn't come without resistance.

Many people believed in me and supported my dream to one day play D1 sports. Still, I also had a large group of people who did not appreciate my aspirations and told me that I was not good enough to make it. "You go to a small high school," they said. "How do you think it will be possible to be good enough and get enough exposure for scouts to notice you?" My detractors tried to make life tough for me, opponents intentionally tried to hurt me in games, people I thought I could trust tried to get me in trouble. These are the kind of responses you can count on from some people when you talk a lot or share too much information. Abraham Lincoln had some wise words on this topic: "Better to remain silent and be thought a fool than to speak out and remove all doubt."

I learned quickly that the best action plan is to be about action. Head down, and grind in silence. Don't worry; they will eventually see the results. You get to save yourself from extra problems when you guard your tongue and talk less.

LET'S PRAY

Dear God,
I want to be a person of action and follow through. I also want to
pay attention to how much I share with others. Please help me to
guard my mouth better when I do choose to speak. Amen.

POSTGAME KEYS

1. What plans or dreams do you have right now?
2. Create an "Outlandish List." This will be a list of crazy, outlandish goals and dreams you have for yourself—things that if someone saw them, they would look at you and ask if you were okay because they seem so far-fetched. Once you're done making your list, store it on your phone, in a journal, or anywhere you can easily access it. Look at it regularly, keep it to yourself, and watch and see what God does or exceeds on that list.
3. Proverbs 21:23 reads, "Those who guard their mouths and their tongues keep themselves from calamity." The choice is yours. What approach will you use as you interact with others?

47   LOVE LIKE GOD

Dear friends, let us love one another, for love comes from God.
Everyone who loves has been born of God and knows God.
Whoever does not love does not know God, because God is love.
1 JOHN 4:7–8

What does it mean to love like God? Do you know what it's like to be loved like God loves? Do you know how God wants us to demonstrate love to others?

Our world is infatuated with "love." We have love songs in almost every single genre of music, and so many films are based on love stories.

Just about everyone desires to have people whom we love—whether that's close friends and family or a soulmate. However, we must be careful how we love. Worldly love gives and receives out of insecurity, out of lack, and from a place of greed and selfishness. We are imperfect humans with bad judgment at times, which increases our chances of making decisions that don't please God and put us in harm's way—a broken heart, injury, mental anguish, or other hurts.

I'm not saying you can't date or be in a relationship because you don't fully know how to love like God. However, I want to set you up for success, because we can never truly know what love is until we experience God's love.

How do we love like God? First, we need to love him! Deuteronomy 6:5 says, "Love the LORD your God with all your heart and with all your soul and with all your strength." We often put our boyfriends, girlfriends, goals, sports, idols, video games, and social media before God, but God should always be number one.

Second, we need to love unconditionally! Unconditional love is caring about someone without limitations, loving without conditions, and doing things to make that person happy without thinking about what we might get in return. This type of love is rare; receiving kindness without strings attached is uncommon, and only God does it perfectly. He is the perfect example of unconditional love and the only one who can show us how to truly love another person. I urge you to read the Bible so you can see how often God puts his unconditional love on display. Read the Gospels—Matthew, Mark, Luke, and John—for a vivid experience of God's love.

In order to practice loving like God, start by serving your teammates, coaches, parents, friends, classmates, coworkers, school, and community. Keep putting God first, do your best to love others like God loves you, and watch the effect of God's love on other people and yourself.

=== **LET'S PRAY**

Dear God,
I want to love like you love, not with conditions and strings
attached. Help change my heart and my views on love, and contin-
ually show me how to love like you love. Amen.

=== **POSTGAME KEYS**

1. Here are five ways you can start loving others like God loves us:

    ▸ **Forgive**—It's a choice, not a feeling. It's on you to forgive.
    ▸ **Be humble**—Humility teaches us that God created us for his purposes, not our own.
    ▸ **Sacrifice**—Put others' needs in front of your own.
    ▸ **Pray**—It's a selfless act to take on others' burdens and increase our faith alongside theirs.
    ▸ **Share**—Share the hope of the gospel with others. It's what we are called to do as Christians—we just happen to be Christians who have a platform.

2. Think of some specific ways you can model God's love to others this week.

3. This Scripture beautifully shares how to love like God: 1 John 4:9–11.

48 GET SMARTER, PLAY SMARTER

Get wisdom, get understanding;
do not forget my words or turn away from them.

Do not forsake wisdom, and she will protect you;
    love her, and she will watch over you.
PROVERBS 4:5–6

What does wisdom mean to you? Would you consider yourself wise or intelligent? How do wisdom and intelligence play a part in your success as an athlete?

I remember playing in a football game and thinking, *Did my brain just rattle inside my skull?* I ran at full speed toward a running back and tackled him. Our helmets collided so hard that I briefly blacked out. By the time I was coherent, I was getting ready to run the next play. I never told my coach, which was foolish because I could have set myself up for further injury. It wasn't until I got older that I realized how precious our brains are and how much we should protect them. Many studies on concussions in sports have shown that damage to the brain can alter our decision-making and cognitive functions.

Our decisions have a significant impact on our lives, which can be temporary or permanent. If you had the opportunity to make the right choices in every situation, would you take it? I'm assuming you would. I want to help you gain wisdom from God so you can make wise decisions and stay ahead of the curve.

The average human being has an average of sixty to seventy thousand thoughts a day. The brain is an incredible organ! Think about everything you can recall. A simple song can take you back in time, as you relive the feelings you felt in that moment. A particular scent can remind you of your childhood.

You use your brain to retain information and to learn new skills in your sport. It's hard for you to be great at your sport without intelligence, which is the ability to acquire and apply knowledge and skills. However, you also need to operate with wisdom, which comes from God himself.

Wisdom comes from humility and a heart that is attuned to God. Wisdom gives you insight into human nature, helps you to understand people and your surroundings better, and enables you to make good decisions because the source of it is divine. When you submit to God's way of life and follow his wisdom, it impacts every area of your life. Being a cerebral athlete is a gift to your game and will elevate you over your competition. However, a cerebral athlete who is also rich in wisdom will outsmart, outwit, and outplay his opponents.

Bring everything to God—all of your decisions, all of your questions. Ask God to give you his wisdom about the people you meet, the schools you visit, the team you join, your future coaches, which camps to attend, the friends in your life, and who you can really trust. Bring everything to God rather than relying on your own intelligence to make decisions. God will give you his wisdom to get smarter and play smarter—in your sport and in life.

=== **LET'S PRAY**

Dear God,
I want to bring everything in my life to you and take the time to listen, obey, and trust you more. Help me to move beyond intelligence to develop true wisdom. Amen.

=== **POSTGAME KEYS**

1. What do you need wisdom about in your life right now? Relationships, decisions, where to go to school, the next step in your sport? Bring all of your concerns to God.

2. If you want wisdom, meditate on this powerful Bible verse: "If you really want to become wise, you must begin by respecting the LORD. To know the Holy One is to gain understanding" (Proverbs 9:10 NIrV).

3. Read Matthew 7:24 this week and let it be your guide. It will help you read the Bible differently.

BUILT DIFFERENT

*Do not conform to the pattern of this world, but be transformed
by the renewing of your mind. Then you will be able to test and
approve what God's will is—his good, pleasing and perfect will.*
ROMANS 12:2

Have you ever felt like you didn't fit in? Do you ever feel like something is
wrong with you? Are you comfortable with feeling different?

Financial guru Dave Ramsey is known for saying, "If you will live like no
one else, later you can live like no one else." These words are also true when
it comes to our faith—when we choose to follow the lifestyle of Jesus and
adopt his ways, we start to live like no one else here on earth, so we can
one day live like no one else in heaven. Sometimes in our culture, you're
not accepted if you're different. On the flip side, there is also a movement
to be über-different from what the masses consider to be normal. However,
neither pertains to what it means to be set apart when you choose to live
a life for Christ.

I've always felt like I didn't quite fit in. I was an athlete who loved
anime, Japanese culture, hip-hop, art, martial arts, boxing, football,
basketball, track, architecture, reading, writing, gaming, and Jesus. All
of these things interest me. When I was younger, I was told I needed to
narrow my interests and focus on just one thing, because focusing in
would allow me to be great at one thing rather than average at many. I
understand the concept, but it's simply not the truth. You may need to
focus on the task at hand or the season you are in so you can excel at

a high level, but that does not mean you need to lose those other interests. When the time is right and the seasons switch, you may have more time and energy to put toward those passions. You *can* have balance in your life.

A lot of people may think you are different or weird because you love Jesus. That's okay. Don't cover it up or worry about what others think. It's actually a compliment. The light within you can be bright, and when you step into the darkness, your light will shine through and pierce the darkness. When you decide to follow Jesus, you are not the one transforming or renewing your own mind. That is God's job. You made the decision to follow him, and he aligns your mind and heart with his. Once you allow that to occur, you can operate in God's perfect will, and his mission can be fulfilled through you.

Be thankful you are built different. You have a purpose. You will change lives through your surrender and obedience to God; sports are just one avenue for God to use you miraculously. Live like no one else, the way God intended you to live.

LET'S PRAY

Dear God,
I'm thankful I'm set apart and different. I realize it's not a bad
thing, but an awesome gift to be different and transformed by you.
Please help me always to appreciate that. Amen.

POSTGAME KEYS

1. Live differently now, so you can live differently later.
2. Do you feel as if you are like everyone else, or do you feel like you are living differently from the world? Figure out how God wants you to live—and then live that way.
3. Remember—it's okay to be different. Own your uniqueness. It's not a mistake that God created you the way he did.

THE HERALD APPROACH

John replied in the words of Isaiah the prophet, "I am the voice of one calling in the wilderness, 'Make straight the way for the Lord.'"
JOHN 1:23

Are your actions a reflection of Jesus? When you are doing well, do you point back to the Lord? Are you letting people know who Jesus is? Do you know who Jesus is?

If you read John 1 all the way to verse 23, you will see that it is John the Baptist's testimony. He was questioned by priests and Levites from Jerusalem and asked, "Who are you? Are you the Savior? Are you Elijah? Are you a prophet? We need to know who you are, so we can go back and report our findings of this mysterious man." John the Baptist said no to all of their questions and simply told them, "I am the voice of one calling in the wilderness, 'Make straight the way for the Lord.'"

John was a herald—a proclaimer, a publicist, the announcer of another person's fame. Imagine someone walking down the street miles ahead of a parade, broadcasting that the president was marching in the parade behind him. "Make sure you get ready!" is what John the Baptist was announcing. He was preparing people for Jesus' arrival by encouraging them to turn from their sins, stressing that they repent and be baptized before Jesus arrived on the scene.

This is our role too. We should share the good news and tell of how he has transformed our lives. We must remember that our accomplishments in sports are not our reward. Jesus is our reward. And, ultimately, it's all about Jesus.

I started reading the Bible because I was tired of secondhand Christianity. My parents would tell me, "Don't do that because the Bible says not to." Or, "Do that because the Bible says you should." I wanted to figure things out for myself. I wanted to know Jesus Christ personally and have my own relationship with him. I often didn't know what to do when I found myself struggling with peer pressure, depression, and insecurity. But when I truly got to know Jesus, I discovered how to respond to those situations. That's when I found out how incredible my purpose is and the gifts God has given me to point others to him.

God called you to be your own unique person even before you were formed in your mother's womb. God called you to be the salt of the earth, to run fast, to sprint ahead and tell people in your sphere of influence that there is someone they have to meet. His name is Jesus Christ, and he will right your wrongs, give you hope in a hopeless society, and turn you and your team upside down in the very best way. Share the message of Jesus with everyone around you. Be a herald.

LET'S PRAY

Dear God,
Please use me to share the good news about who you are and what
you can do for people. Help me to remember to point back to you
with my life and my actions. Amen.

POSTGAME KEYS

1. Think of some ways you can share the gospel with your teammates or others through your words or actions.
2. Reflect on this question: Would people know you are a Christian by your actions if you never told them? If the answer is no, write down some changes you can make in your life.
3. Mark 16:15 makes it clear that we need to share the gospel with as many people as possible. Let this Scripture motivate you to share the good news.

51 IT JUST TAKES ONE PLAY

This is the message we have heard from him and declare to you: God is light; in him there is no darkness at all.
1 JOHN 1:5

PREGAME

Do you feel comfortable telling people about Jesus? If not, why do you think that is? Can you recall a time when someone spoke to you about Jesus?

GAME TIME

Sales companies love to recruit athletes because most athletes are driven by competition and seem to hate losing even more than they like winning. When I worked at Verizon Wireless and the Apple Store, I made it a point to try to be the top salesperson at my store. If you were the top seller, I was coming for you, and my coworkers knew it. They knew it because of my on-floor hustle and the numbers I was putting up. I prided myself on being a "silent assassin." But be aware of how you come across—especially if you love to win. You never know who is paying attention to you and watching how you carry yourself.

You can still be competitive and live for Jesus. During many of my work breaks, I spent time studying my Bible or reading a book. I prayed before I ate. I did not curse in conversations. I had fun but didn't feel the need to drink at work parties.

All those actions added up to one moment.

One day I walked to the back offices to ask a coworker about a client we had acquired. When I approached him, I noticed he wasn't acting like himself. I asked him if he was okay, and he told me he wasn't. He then shared with me that he and his wife had been in the process of getting a divorce because she had cheated on him. He also told me his wife had gone to a party where she overdosed and didn't make it. He was carrying all of that pain inside and had not shared it with anyone else at work.

I knew he was an atheist, but I asked him anyway, "Can I pray for you?" He surprised me by saying he didn't mind. We went outside the store to get some privacy, and I started to pray. During the prayer, he burst into tears and hugged me, and I finished the prayer with him in my arms. He told me he knew I was a real Christian because he saw my actions and noticed a light about me. That was God's light, not my own.

God used this one moment to reroute my coworker's life. He went to church for the first time and then started attending. Friends, it only takes one play to change someone's life forever. Just like all the preparation during the off-season, training camp, in-season practices, and conditioning can come down to just one play to win the championship, the same is true in the Christian life.

You never know when God wants to use you. It can be an intimate moment or on a national platform. Either way, remember that it takes just one play. Prepare now to be used by God in the moments that count.

LET'S PRAY

Dear God,
Help me to love the things you love and hate the things you hate so
I can be used by you. Please shine your light through me so others
can be reached. Amen.

POSTGAME KEYS

1. Ask God to keep you prepared to pray for someone who needs God's love and wisdom in their life.
2. Notice how you spend your time and remember that others are watching you.
3. Take time to learn about God and meditate on his Word for yourself so you are ready in and out of season to share the goodness of God with others.

For to us a child is born,
to us a son is given,
and the government will be on his shoulders.
And he will be called
Wonderful Counselor, Mighty God,
Everlasting Father, Prince of Peace.
ISAIAH 9:6

PREGAME

Who is your favorite athlete, and why? What do you find admirable about them? Do you personally know how amazing Jesus is? Do you ever talk about him?

GAME TIME

If those pregame questions challenged you, that is a good thing. I hope you walk away from this devotional inspired to open up your Bible and read it with a coachable athlete's mentality, so you can get to know our heavenly Father better and understand why he is such a big deal. Jesus is the ultimate flex. There is nothing or no one bigger than Jesus. He is the Wonderful Counselor, Mighty God, Everlasting Father, Prince of Peace, Creator, Savior, and King of kings.

Have you ever stood next to someone who is smoking a cigarette? I can't stand the thought of inhaling so many toxins from their secondhand smoke—without actually smoking! I've been tempted to slap the cigarette out of their hand and tell them how lethal cigarettes are, but clearly, that's not the right choice. However, I won't allow someone else to damage my body, even if they don't care about their own body.

Did you know that you can also die spiritually from "secondhand Christianity"? Parents, leaders, coaches, and teammates might tell you things you shouldn't do because the Bible says not to do them, but if you have never read God's Word for yourself, you won't feel personally convicted. For example, have you been told you shouldn't have premarital sex? There is a reason why so many Scriptures warn you not to be sexually immoral and that rather than burn with sexual desire, you should get married. God knows what he is saving you from. He knows the heartache, drama, diseases, and pain you can sidestep. So many people have died spiritually from secondhand Christianity—they were told not to do something but never read the Word for themselves to have the Holy Spirit speak to their hearts and show them how to live.

The Bible is not a book of rules; it's a spiritual GPS for your life. It allows you to get to know the God we serve intimately. You will find out what gives your life meaning, discover his ultimate plan, read about his promises, and so much more. And, maybe best of all, you can apply the Bible's principles to your everyday life and sport.

Many of the difficulties Christians experience can be traced back to a lack of Bible study and reading. Don't put all the pressure on your chaplain, pastor, or youth leader to teach you the Bible. Learn about and experience God for yourself, and I promise your life will never be the same. You'll discover why Jesus is such a big deal, and you'll be inspired to talk more about him.

LET'S PRAY

Dear God,
Please help me as I embark on a journey of getting to know you
for myself. Reveal yourself to me and teach me how to be like you.
Then help me to talk about you—especially when I feel like talking
about myself. Amen.

POSTGAME KEYS

1. If you have yet to choose a Bible you can understand, do so this week. I'm excited for you to get a new study Bible and start learning from it. Decide how you want to use your Bible and what features

you need. Then choose a translation that is accurate and easy to understand. Ask God to help you make your choice.

2. Because different study Bibles have different purposes, take time to think about whether you need a study Bible whose focus is on providing information to help in your understanding or one whose goal is to give guidance for applying the Bible to your daily life.

3. Your personal relationship with God is the most important part of your journey. Fall in love with studying the Bible for yourself.

STUDY YOUR PLAYBOOK

Keep this Book of the Law always on your lips; meditate on it day and night, so that you may be careful to do everything written in it. Then you will be prosperous and successful.
JOSHUA 1:8

PREGAME

Do you like to study? What's the best way for you to learn something? Are you a visual, auditory, kinesthetic, or reading/writing learner?

GAME TIME

During two-a-day football camp in high school, coaches handed out playbooks and told each player to study it and know it inside out. You can tell when something is important by how someone speaks about it and the tone they use. I figured out quickly that if I didn't study that playbook, there would be repercussions. If I didn't learn that playbook, I would ruin my chances of playing. And it makes sense. How can a coach or teammate trust a player who is unwilling to put in the effort to learn the team's philosophies and plans? It shows laziness if we are not willing to take the time to prioritize the playbook.

The Bible is similar to a playbook, yet on a grander scale. But it's not just a book of knowledge and rules. It's a living book that instructs us on how to conduct ourselves in challenging situations, live like Christ, and understand how historical events are relevant to us today. The words of Joshua 1:8 hold much weight—memorizing and meditating on God's Word will make us prosperous and successful.

Did you know that you should chew your food between thirty-two and forty times per bite to break it down properly? The goal is for your body to eventually extract the nutrients from what you are eating after it goes down your esophagus and into your stomach. This process of digestion is similar to how we are to study our Bible. We aren't supposed to skim over Scripture. We are to take our time with it, dissecting it and considering it. We are to meditate on it and think about it repeatedly, as if we were chewing on a piece of steak that may take forty bites to break down.

Study the Bible like you would study the most important playbook ever. When you discover and learn the Bible on a deeper level, you can apply it to the fabric of your life and your soul, transforming you from the inside out to be more like Christ. Take your time when you read the Bible. Remember, it's not just a book you read but a supernatural guide to navigating life and being a better athlete, a better teammate, and, most importantly, a better person.

LET'S PRAY

Dear God,
Thank you for giving us the playbook to life. Help me fall in love
with reading my Bible and give me the desire to study it with a
passion to be transformed from within. Amen.

POSTGAME KEYS

1. Figure out what style of learning helps you retain information the easiest. Then, apply it to your Bible reading. You can try multiple ways of learning to digest what the Bible is saying. Sometimes it helps to mix things up–listen to Scripture on audio, watch

something like *The Chosen*, read it for yourself, listen to worship songs based on Scripture.

2. Romans 10:17 says, "Faith comes from hearing the message, and the message is heard through the word about Christ."

3. The Bible is the most important playbook you will ever have to study. This is the true key to life.

SPIRITUAL SHOWER

Create in me a pure heart, O God,
and renew a steadfast spirit within me.
PSALM 51:10

PREGAME

Do you ever feel like you messed up and wish you could have a fresh start? Do you feel you have a better attitude some days than others? What do you think is the key to having a good attitude and a positive mindset?

GAME TIME

So many distractions keep us from spending time with God. We juggle sports, school, work, everyday life, friends, pressures, current events, illnesses—the list goes on and on. The longer we go without spending time with God, the easier it becomes for us to stink spiritually. Our patience grows thin, our attitude worsens, our decision-making lacks conviction, and we let slide things we would normally stay on top of. We need God's Word daily to cleanse us and keep us holy. We can't do this life on our own—we are simply not strong enough, no matter how physically and mentally tough we think we are as athletes.

We live in an informational age where anything we need to know is at our fingertips.

If you want to find the nearest restaurant, there's an app for that!

If you want to discover the latest sports scores, there's an app for that!

If you want more information about a potential school or team, there's an app for that!

If you want directions to a destination, there's an app for that!

If you want to track your calories, there's an app for that!

If you want to download books, there's an app for that!

If you want to play games, there's an app for that!

If you want to change your life, the Bible can do that!

If you are feeling down and need a pick-me-up, there's a Bible passage that will encourage you!

If your heart is weary and in pain, there's a Bible passage that will lift you up!

If you have lost your fire for God, there's a Bible passage that will inspire you!

If you are lonely, there's a Bible passage that will give you hope!

If you want to be the voice for your generation and impact your world for Jesus Christ, there's a Bible passage that will spur you on!

Yes, the Scriptures are truly that powerful. They will change you from the inside out when you open up the Word and ask God to speak to you.

Take time as David did in Psalm 51:10 and ask God to give you a clean heart and renew a steadfast spirit within you. If you feel as if you have lost your zeal or joy for the Lord, ask God to ignite that spark inside of you so you can be used the way he wants to use you today.

LET'S PRAY

Dear God,
I want to take a spiritual shower daily by spending time with you and reading your Word. Please help me to make this a lifestyle. Amen.

POSTGAME KEYS

1. Try to recall the last time you had a spiritual shower. If it's been a while, make sure you find time to cleanse yourself with God's Word on a regular basis. Be intentional about staying connected

to God every day. Schedule time to pray, read your Bible, and hang out with the Lord.

2. God wants to be present in your life daily.

3. Continue to ask God daily for a renewed, refreshed, and repentant heart.

TOUGH LOVE

Whoever claims to love God yet hates a brother or sister is a liar. For whoever does not love their brother and sister, whom they have seen, cannot love God, whom they have not seen.
1 JOHN 4:20

PREGAME

Would you consider yourself to be a person who has good self-control? Or do you find yourself losing your temper often? How do you respond when someone pushes your buttons and makes you mad?

GAME TIME

Teammates can sometimes be brutal toward each other, but it's usually all in fun. Unfortunately, things can sometimes escalate until someone crosses the line and it becomes dangerous. There was a week in college when team pranks started to get out of hand. I came to practice late one day because I had to take a test, which my coaches knew beforehand. When I got to my locker, I was in a hurry because I didn't want to get too far behind in practice. As I changed into my football girdle and put on my pads, it felt like my groin area was catching on fire. The more I moved, the hotter it felt. I continued putting on my football equipment, grabbed my helmet, and jogged out of the locker room—and then it clicked. The burning sensation was Icy Hot, and I was not happy about it.

When I got to the practice field, I could tell that some teammates knew what was happening, and they were looking for my reaction. One of my teammates even asked me how my groin felt, and I immediately knew he was in on it. However, I did my best not to show any emotion at all.

After that, all I could see was red. I was angry with him, and I could not shake it. I was on a mission to get him back.

I wish I could tell you that I read or remembered 1 John 4:20 and it changed my heart in that moment, but because I wasn't reading my Bible daily or spending as much time with God as I should have been, it affected my actions. I ended up getting my teammate back, and it turned into a pretty nasty war that almost got me kicked off the football team. I saw a quote by Confucius that struck me hard: "Before you embark on a journey of revenge, dig two graves."

This quote has a lot of truth in it because, believe it or not, revenge hurts both sides. It may feel good in the moment, but it impacts your soul negatively while hurting the person you're targeting and possibly innocent people.

We can't claim to be Christian athletes and pick and choose how we want to live. The Christian walk isn't easy, and sometimes you don't feel like being like Jesus. However, it's one thing to quote Scriptures, call yourself a Christian, and read the Bible, but what good is all that if you don't live your life according to God's Word? That's why John says we can't truly love a God we can't see if we hate a brother or sister whom we can see. God challenges us to always love others, even when it's tough.

LET'S PRAY

Dear God,
I want to be a conduit of your love. Help me rise above my flesh
and be more like you and treat others with love, no matter how
they treat me. Amen.

POSTGAME KEYS

1. When you feel angry with someone and want to respond by getting revenge, ask yourself, *Would people see God through me if I were to do this?*

2. You have the opportunity to be someone else's experience of our loving God.

3. Try this before you want to react and get someone back:

   ▸ Ask yourself, *Would God approve of my intended actions?*
   ▸ Ask yourself, *Is this worth getting in trouble for and ruining my future?*
   ▸ Take a deep breath and pray for the person who wronged you.
   ▸ Let God fight your battle—turn your back on the situation, and be the better person. Take to heart these words from Exodus 14:14: "The LORD will fight for you; you need only to be still."

56　YOU CAN'T EARN THIS

Do you not know that in a race all the runners run, but only one gets the prize? Run in such a way as to get the prize. Everyone who competes in the games goes into strict training. They do it to get a crown that will not last, but we do it to get a crown that will last forever.
1 CORINTHIANS 9:24–25

PREGAME

How do you prepare to compete? What keeps you focused on your goal? Are you aware that there are heavenly rewards?

GAME TIME

To win, you have to compete. You must commit to a lifestyle of discipline, consistency, hard work, patience, resilience, toughness, and dedication. Elite athletes will do what is necessary to rise to the top and commit to doing things that average athletes won't do—for example, eating the right foods to fuel their bodies, not partaking in drugs, not participating in activities that could get them hurt, getting ample sleep and rest, making sure they recover after hard workouts, and working to keep their mental health strong.

This is also true about how we should approach our pursuit of Christian living. The difference is that we don't earn our way into heaven. Eternal life is a gift from God through the death and resurrection of Jesus Christ, which we accept by faith. However, we still need to apply the tenacity of a great athlete toward our pursuit of the eternal prize. By improving our knowledge of God's Word and by meditating on it day and night, we will be able to understand what the Bible says and then apply it to our lives.

Just like we train for the opponents we compete against, we have to train to battle spiritual adversaries. We must fight against the devil's schemes, as well as our own past issues, iniquities, triggers, and anything that tries to trip us up. Sometimes we may fall, slip up, and struggle, but just like my defensive coach would say, we need to play with short-term memory. Though we may have gotten burned in the previous play, we can't let it keep us from moving on and giving our all in the next play.

We will be tempted to quit and give up. We may be tempted to cheat, cut corners, and not work as hard as we should. But hold this verse near to your heart. James 1:12 says, "Blessed is the one who perseveres under trial because, having stood the test, that person will receive the crown of life that the Lord has promised to those who love him." With this type of spiritual training, you will be prepared to win on earth and receive your reward in heaven.

=== **LET'S PRAY**

Dear God,
I want to think past just my earthly gain. Please help me to keep
my eyes focused on my spiritual reward. Help me to compete with
an eternal mindset. Amen.

1. Here are a few Scriptures referencing some of our rewards in heaven:

   For what is our hope, our joy, or the crown in which we will glory in the presence of our Lord Jesus when he comes? Is it not you? (1 Thessalonians 2:19)

   Now there is in store for me the crown of righteousness, which the Lord, the righteous Judge, will award to me on that day—and not only to me, but also to all who have longed for his appearing. (2 Timothy 4:8)

   And when the Chief Shepherd appears, you will receive the crown of glory that will never fade away. (1 Peter 5:4)

2. We need to apply the same game-winning efforts toward our pursuit of the eternal prize, by improving our knowledge of the Word of God and by consistently scheduling time each day to read and meditate on Scripture.
3. When you feel like giving up or quitting, remind yourself that you are an overcomer, resilient, made in the image of God, poised, levelheaded, and rooted in Christ.

57   ARE YOU CHANGED?

Therefore, if anyone is in Christ, the new creation has come: The old has gone, the new is here!
2 CORINTHIANS 5:17

 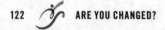

How did you feel when you gave your life to Christ? Did you feel different? If you haven't given your life to Christ yet and you are thinking about doing it, do you expect to feel a change when you do?

Have you ever seen videos of kids and adults who hear sound for the very first time? You can visibly see the transformation on their faces when they begin to hear sounds and words. They are no longer the same after that.

Likewise, we should never be the same after we accept Jesus into our lives. We should not want to go back to our old ways of living life or to being enslaved by sin. You should want to get to know your Creator and figure out what he loves and what he hates and why. When we decide to live for Jesus, a spiritual transformation starts to take place within us.

You may have had a tumultuous past. You are now renewed.

You may have done things you aren't proud of. You are now renewed.

You may have said things that hurt others. You are now renewed.

You may have come from a tough upbringing. You are now renewed.

You may not have believed in Jesus and claimed to be an atheist. You are now renewed.

You may have lived a life gripped in the hands of sin. You are now renewed.

Just because other athletes live in a way that is fulfilling to the flesh does not mean you should follow suit. As a believer in Christ, you are now sanctified, set apart, and declared holy. You are kingdom royalty. Going back to living a life of sin after being born again is like trying to take residence back inside your mother's womb. It doesn't make sense. Be thankful that the old you has gone away and the new you has arrived. Be confident in the new you, and let God continue to change and use you.

Dear God,
I want to experience real change in my life. I want to be renewed
and live a life that is pleasing to you, and I want to inspire others to
want the same thing. Amen.

1. If you gave your life to Christ in the past but feel you have gone backward with your relationship and walk with the Lord, that's okay. Take this time to tell God you want to rededicate your life to him and ask for a renewed relationship with him.

2. If you have never given your life to Christ and want the change you just read about, repeat this prayer out loud:

   Lord Jesus, I humbly come to you right now. I know I am a sinner
   and often fall short of what is pleasing to you. I no longer want to
   live my life absent from you. By faith, I receive your gift of salvation.
   I'm ready to trust you wholeheartedly as my Lord and Savior. I
   believe you came to this earth as the Son of God who died on the
   cross for my sins and rose from the dead. Thank you for forgiving
   me of my sins and giving me eternal life. Jesus, I invite you to come
   into my heart and be my Savior. Amen.

   Congratulations on making the GREATEST DECISION of your life!

3. Memorize Jeremiah 29:11 and study Ephesians 5:1–2.

58   TAKE IT ALL IN

Therefore do not worry about tomorrow, for tomorrow will
worry about itself. Each day has enough trouble of its own.
MATTHEW 6:34

How often do you appreciate the moment you are in? Are you capturing the moment for your own memories or for social media?

My dad always gave me wise advice whenever I was preparing to go on a college visit to listen to recruiting offers. He told me to soak in every moment of those trips. Not everyone has the opportunity to experience being courted by multiple universities, each one trying to convince you that you should choose their school. It's okay to take pictures and videos to document the process, but remember that the moments you experience while being fully present will never leave you. Capturing content to share on social media is awesome, but experiencing the present is a gift you can never get back.

I had the privilege of bringing my parents along with me on those visits, and I'm so glad I did because we made memories I will never forget. I remember worrying if a particular school would still want to offer me a scholarship when I got there. My father would remind me to enjoy the process and cherish the moment.

Whenever a school shared its major pitch at dinner and asked, "Will you choose to play for us?" my dad and I excused ourselves and went into the bathroom to talk about the pros and cons and to put on the table any concerns I was having about the program, the location and look of the campus, the demographics, the feel of the players, the vibe of the coaches, the appeal of the stadium, the quality of the curriculum, and the way my parents and I felt as we soaked up the environment.

It would have been easy to concentrate on documenting the experience, but God has a different plan for how we go through life. Don't let the enemy steal your joy by filling you with worry and distracting you from the present.

Transition to a new phase of life can be exciting and scary at the same time. Leaving high school for college is a big step in gaining responsibility for your own decisions. Moving to the next season of your life can breed insecurities, and questions arise in your mind:

Will a school recruit you?

Will you get drafted?

Will you play your sport for a long time?

Will you earn a starting position?

Will your teammates like you?

Will your coaches like you?

Will the fans love you?

Will you get drafted into the professional sports world?

Will you need to think about transitioning into the workforce?

These are all valid things to think about. This is where our trust in God is important because our faith will be tested. Do you believe God is in control? If you do, will you trust him when you can't see the finish line? Be present in the moments during these crucial years of your life instead of looking ahead to the next phase and how to get there, because ultimately God is in control. You can try to manipulate details and work things out for yourself, but ultimately God is at the wheel. He has already written your story. Trust him fully, and let tomorrow worry about itself.

LET'S PRAY

Dear God,
Help me to focus on living for you and fully enjoying the present. Please give me the strength to trust that you are in control and that I don't need to worry because you have my best interests at heart. Amen.

POSTGAME KEYS

1. Try to be intentional about being in the moment the next time you go on vacation, play in a big game, take part in a tournament, get together with friends, hang out with your teammates, or spend time with God through prayer and reading his Word.

2. Stop trying to delete, edit, or revise your life. Give God your worry, and let him work everything out.

 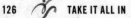

3. Read Psalm 34:4 and Psalm 94:19 to help you worry less and remind you to let God be in control.

AFTER YOU'RE DONE PLAYING

Plans fail for lack of counsel,
but with many advisers they succeed.
PROVERBS 15:22

PREGAME

Are you a planner? Do you think about what your future will look like after you are finished playing your sport? What are your plans for that time?

GAME TIME

There will come a day when you cannot play your sport at the level you are playing now. Some athletes can play their sport for a long time—just ask some golfers—but rugby, football, or hockey might be hard to play when you're well into your sixties. You need to have a plan. Formulating a graceful exit from your sport is in your best interest. It is wise to find knowledgeable advisers to help you prepare for the future.

During my senior year of college, I reached out to my parents to let them know I was planning to move to San Diego after graduation. I knew they had my best interests at heart, and I knew they would give me good spiritual guidance. They told me to connect with other Christians and get plugged into a church as soon as I could because it would give me a solid foundation and provide accountability as I found my footing in a new place.

I immediately contacted friends in sunny San Diego. I asked about churches and where I could find Christian roommates. A transition of this magnitude can be jarring and stressful without godly advice and direction. It already felt strange because my life was no longer structured for me through school and sports. It was a reality I had to come to grips with, and I'm thankful I proactively had reached out to my parents for godly wisdom. It set me up for a smooth transition into my new season of life, with new Christian roommates and a new church to attend in my new city.

You may not yet be close to that season of life. However, I want you to get ahead of the game and plan for the future. I want you to have wise leaders in your life—people you can trust to give you good advice. We make more mistakes without wise counsel in our lives, and this is why we need to seek out solid advisers who align with God.

Ask God for spiritual wisdom and guidance on those you choose to let speak into your life. Ask the Holy Spirit to lead you in all your decisions because not every Christian leader will give you the advice you need. The Holy Spirit will help you discern what is and isn't applicable in your life.

LET'S PRAY

Dear God,
I'm thankful you care so much for me and my future that you have
put people in my life who will help guide me on my journey. Please
give me the humility to listen to them. Amen.

POSTGAME KEYS

1. Who in your life can you talk to about important decisions you need to make? If it isn't already, put their contact info in your phone so you can reach them when something comes up.
2. Write out a list of things you are passionate about and occupations you would love to do if you were not playing your sport. Keep this list in your phone or on a notepad and keep adding to it. Having it there helps remind you of the things you love and enjoy and could see yourself doing one day.
3. Start planning now to set yourself up for success in the future.

60 LEAVE HIM OUT OF NOTHING

Trust in the LORD with all your heart
and lean not on your own understanding;
in all your ways submit to him,
and he will make your paths straight.

PROVERBS 3:5–6

─── **PREGAME**

Would you say that God is in everything you do? Do you include him in your everyday tasks, workouts, games, matches, competitions, and interactions with other people?

─── **GAME TIME**

Our family loves to collect sports cards. Sometimes, we buy boxes of cards with individual packs within them and split them between us. Then we write the numbers one through five on individual pieces of paper and put them into a hat. Each of us gets to pick a piece of paper, and we open the packs in that order.

When I tell you that I leave God out of nothing, I mean it. I even pray quickly before I stick my hand into the hat to choose my number! It probably sounds trivial, but I try to include God in everything I do because I want to be accustomed to him being part of every area of my life. The Hebrew word for *trust* is *batach*, which means "to entrust yourself to, hope in, put your entire weight on something." When you sit on a ledge, you trust with all your weight that it will not give way and will be safe for you to sit on. That's *batach*.

God wants us to trust him with all of our hearts and leave him out of nothing. As Christian athletes, we realize that Jesus paid the ultimate price for our sins, and when we choose to live for him, we involve him in everything—including the sport we play. We don't pick and choose where God should be in our lives—he should always be in the center.

Here's an example of how this works: Picture a delicious German chocolate cake with coconut pecan frosting. This chocolate cake represents God. When I cut the cake, each slice represents the various things you do—your sport, school, hobbies, work, family, friends, church, and community service. No matter which slice you select, it's still chocolate cake with coconut pecan frosting.

This is how we should live our lives, with God at the center of each slice and with complete trust that he will make our paths straight. When we rely on our own understanding and try to make our own plans, we tend to increase the adversity in our lives. But when we include God in every part of our lives, we enhance our joy by bringing glory to the Lord and allowing him to make our paths straight.

LET'S PRAY

Dear God,
I don't want you to be excluded from any area of my life. If you see
an area where you're not involved, please reveal that place to me
and set up camp there. Amen.

POSTGAME KEYS

1. We make better decisions when God is at the center of our lives.
2. Think of some areas where you are not including God in your life and ask him to be a part of those places and situations.
3. Write Proverbs 3:5–6 on a sticky note or index card and put it up in a high-traffic area so you can memorize it and be reminded to include God in every part of your life.

61

Love one another with brotherly affection.
Outdo one another in showing honor.
ROMANS 12:10 ESV

PREGAME

Do you treat certain people differently than others? Or do you try to treat everyone equally, regardless of status, race, or gender? Do you feel like you are treated fairly?

GAME TIME

The Seattle Seahawks organization is comprised of a special group of individuals who give five-star treatment to their guests. I have had the privilege and honor to experience firsthand many athletic organizations and top-tier companies. When I first stepped into the Virginia Mason Athletic Center in Renton, Washington—the headquarters of the Seattle Seahawks—my wife and I were treated with love, respect, kindness, luxury, and a feeling of worth. It didn't matter if you were talking to President Chuck Arnold, General Manager John Schneider, Head Coach Pete Carroll, the players, the training staff, the community outreach team, the social media team, the chefs, the janitors, or the security staff. Everyone treated everyone else with kindness, respect, and love.

It feels like the Seahawks try to outdo each other in treating people with honor. This is the culture that upper management has set within the organization. Like the Seahawks organization, we, as followers of Christ, can give people this same kind of five-star treatment. Paul shares in Romans 12:10 what it means to be a self-sacrificing Christian. Our heart, mission, and goal should be to make everyone, regardless of status, race, or gender, feel equally honored.

The reality is that you won't like everyone, but the way you treat people will be a great indicator of how much love you have for Jesus. If your heart is full of love, it will spill out onto others effortlessly. We can't pour water from an empty cup. We need to spend time with God in prayer, worship, and reading and hearing the Bible so we can overflow with the love of Jesus.

Imagine if you took your competitiveness and applied it to outdoing others. What if you set the standard of giving the most honor to others and treating people with the most love. You will change the dynamic of your team culture and community. Have a five-star mentality of offering everyone your absolute best.

LET'S PRAY

Dear God,
I want to have a heart that treats everyone I meet equally with love
and honor. Help me to love others with your love, even when I have
trouble liking or relating to them. Amen.

POSTGAME KEYS

1. Think of how you treat the people in your life, and make sure you treat each one of them equally and with honor.
2. Let God use you to love and honor people. Make a list of three people you feel you could honor better.
3. Here are two Scriptures for you to reference on how to treat others in a godly way: Luke 6:31 and Matthew 6:14–15.

62   DO YOUR PART, WATCH GOD DO HIS

When a person's ways please the LORD,
he makes even his enemies to be at peace with him.
PROVERBS 16:7 CSB

Have you ever had people not like you? Do you have any enemies? If you do, why do you think that is?

It doesn't feel good when someone lies about you or throws shade your way. When I was a sophomore in college, certain teammates of mine were lying about my character to a girl in order to sway her view of me. The situation was hurtful because they were teammates I thought of like brothers and the girl was a friend I knew from back home. She and I were close. I knew her family, and our families were friends. I was a sophomore, and she was an incoming freshman. When people found out we knew each other, my teammates started sharing information with her about me that wasn't true. I noticed my friendship with her began to change, and when I found out it was because of my teammates, I wanted to confront them—and not in a positive way—until I attended a Bible study on campus, and we discussed this Scripture:

> When a person's ways please the LORD,
> he makes even his enemies to be at peace with him.

This verse arrived right on time, just like it may be arriving now for you. I was reminded that if I wanted my life to improve, I needed to ensure my relationship with God and my intentions and actions were good. Other people's issues are not our battles to fight. God knows our hearts and our thinking and sees our actions. If they are not pleasing to the Lord, we can get in the way of God's blessing on our lives. However, when we make sure our lives align with God's plan and we do our part to please him, we can witness the supernatural.

What the enemy may have set up for your downfall, God can redeem for your success and his glory. It may not be immediate, but when it comes to pass, you will know it's from God. As I write this devotional, I see how he redeemed that extremely tough situation from college by blessing me with an opportunity to share the story with you and give him the glory. If I had acted on my own, I could have ruined my life. But now, I get to tell you that God sees you, loves you, knows your situation, and wants to bless you. Just align yourself with him, make sure your actions are pleasing to him, and let him work out the rest. Do your part, and then watch God do his.

LET'S PRAY

Dear God,
Thank you for your mercy and grace over my life. Today I want to align myself with you and make sure my actions are pleasing to you. Amen.

POSTGAME KEYS

1. On a daily basis, take stock of your actions and ask yourself if they are pleasing to God.
2. Meditate on Proverbs 16:7 this week and let God's Word shape and guide your actions.
3. Remember, when we give our lives to God we become a new creation. Read Galatians 2:20 this week.

63 GATHER WITH OTHERS

Therefore encourage one another and build each other up, just as in fact you are doing.
1 THESSALONIANS 5:11

PREGAME

Who do you meet with to talk about the Bible? Do you have any teammates or friends you can gather with to pray and worship? Is there someone in your life with whom you can study the Bible?

My relationship with God grew deeper when I hung out with other believers and teammates who wanted to pray, read the Bible, and talk together about our discoveries. I knew it was important to spend time with other Christians, but I didn't exactly know why. I did it because I grew up in a household where my parents were pastors, and it was never an option *not* to go to church. I was very thankful for the upbringing I had, but I didn't always realize how blessed I was to have it.

The light bulb went off for me when I decided to attend Bible studies with other Christian athletes. When we read the same Scriptures together, it was awesome to hear different perspectives on the same passages. I discovered for myself how reading the Bible and discussing it helps you to understand it and apply it to your life. God doesn't want us to live the Christian life on our own. We are meant to build each other up and help one another on our journey as followers of Christ.

If you play on a team, you understand that when we compete against each other in practice, we make each other better. The competition isn't to minimize each other but to help us improve our skills and reach our goals. As a team, if we don't get on the same page, or if we take on an individualistic mindset, we will fall apart. When we are aligned, we have a better chance to succeed and win games. If you play an individual sport, you enhance your chances of doing well if you and your coaches are united on your training and preparation.

In the game of life, we are to improve our knowledge of God, strengthen our relationship with him, and tell others the good news. Hebrews 10:24–25 says, "And let us consider how we may spur one another on toward love and good deeds, not giving up meeting together, as some are in the habit of doing, but encouraging one another—and all the more as you see the Day approaching." I challenge you to step up and be the leader of your team and gather other Christians to connect with, as all of you get to know God on a more intimate level. Through these actions, you can be a light for your teammates and others who may not know Jesus yet.

Dear God,
I want to learn more about you with my teammates or fellow
athletes. I realize we are meant to live in community with other
believers. Help me find the right friends with whom I can pray,
worship, and learn about you. Amen.

================================== **POSTGAME KEYS**

1. If you are not connected to a church yet, make it a priority to find one. You might want to look for a church with a Bible study for people in your age group or stage of life.
2. If your team has a team chaplain, make it a point to connect with them. If the chaplain runs a Bible study, make it a point to participate in it.
3. If your team doesn't offer a Bible study, pray about starting one with your teammates.

64   GO NORTH!

Produce fruit in keeping with repentance.
MATTHEW 3:8

================================== **PREGAME**

Have you ever heard of repentance? What does repentance mean to you?

================================== **GAME TIME**

As a young running back, I used to love making people miss. My goal was to snatch a defender's ankles from them by juking side to side till I would make them overcommit, and then I would run the opposite way while they collected the pieces of their dignity and pride from the turf. As I got older, it drove my coaches nuts. All I heard from my coach was,

"Stop going east, west, and south. Just go north!" His logic was that I wasted precious time juking defenders because, by the time I made all those moves, more defenders were on their way to tackle me, which was true. He wanted me to eliminate moves that weren't necessary and run as quickly as possible.

Over time my progression, skills, and yardage improved, because I minimized going backward and taking extra steps that often got me in trouble with defenders. It was a habit I had to learn to improve. I would tell my coach, "Yes, I gotcha." But my actions displayed something else. When I got into those familiar situations, my instincts took over and I sometimes returned to my old ways. But it always cost me better stats and sometimes lost me playing time.

We tend to act the same way with the sin that's in our lives. We know we shouldn't do something, yet we do it anyway—and then we need to change our ways and repent. The word *repentance* comes from the Jewish word *teshuvah*, which means "turning back to God, changing our minds, turning our backs to sin, running toward God." The goal with repentance is not only to feel bad about the action we committed and say we repent of the sin, but also to turn our back on that action and turn toward God.

God wants our actions to be the fruit of repentance, which means that if we say we repent, our actions will demonstrate that decision. We need to recognize our sin and feel remorse, which should spur us on to repentance. We will make mistakes, and we will fall short of the goal. However, the more we learn from God and the Bible, the better we can apply his direction to our everyday lives. You will always be tempted. The more you say no and truly repent, the easier it becomes to "go north!" Don't return to your old ways. Turn your back on sin and run toward God.

LET'S PRAY

Dear God,
I want to learn to repent with my actions, not just with my words.
Please help me to do that as I turn my back to sin and turn toward
you. Amen.

1. Think of a way you've sinned today or this week. Ask God to help you with your repentance process.
2. Read Matthew 3:10, and also meditate on Matthew 3:8 this week.
3. Ask yourself this question as you go about your day: *Am I producing good fruit?*

APPRECIATE EVERYTHING

I will give thanks to you, LORD, with all my heart;
I will tell of all your wonderful deeds.
PSALM 9:1

Can you honestly say you appreciate everything? Could you imagine being so confident in God that you thank him even in the tough times?

It's easy to take the credit when things are going well. Even then, do you appreciate your blessings? Do you appreciate that not everyone gets to play a sport?

If you are chosen to be on the team, that is a blessing.

If you can play in a game and compete, that is a blessing.

If you compete in a game and win—or lose—that is a blessing.

If you compete, get hurt, and are still alive, with a chance to recover, that is a blessing.

If you are good enough to be recruited by a university, that is a blessing.

If you get to play just for the joy of it, that is a blessing.

It is a blessing if you are reading this right now because you are alive. This is your reminder to appreciate everything you are experiencing. Take a moment and give God the glory for your gifts and talents, as well as for the air in your lungs and the energy in your body. In the Bible, David had power, clout, authority, influence, and notoriety, but he chose to brag in God's name, take no credit for himself, and keep God in the number one spot in his life. If we have this same attitude, we will better appreciate everything because we realize it's not about us; it's about what God has blessed us with.

================================ LET'S PRAY

Dear God,
Help me to appreciate everything in my life, even if things do not
go my way. Remind me that you are in control and it's for my own
good. Amen.

=============================== POSTGAME KEYS

1. Think about what you are going through, or what you have experienced recently, and express your appreciation for all the ways God has blessed you.
2. Take time this week to appreciate moments on the field, on the court, on the track, on the mat, in the pool, or in the ring. Appreciate the beauty of creation, the roof over your head, your health, the opportunities you have, your family, your teammates, your coaches, and those who support you.
3. Start your mornings with 1 Chronicles 29:13 this week. Let prayer and praise become a natural habit.

66 YOUR LIFE IS WORTH LIVING

No one will be able to stand against you all the days of your life. As I was with Moses, so I will be with you; I will never leave you nor forsake you.
JOSHUA 1:5

Do you believe you have worth? Do you believe God will never leave you in the good or in the tough times? How do you deal with the stresses of life?

I remember finally moving into my dorm room in Peabody Hall in Miami, Ohio, at the end of football two-a-days. Unpacking my clothes, setting up my new computer, meeting my new roommates, and connecting with other athletes on campus was surreal. My excitement to start classes was at an all-time high, but as I picked up the books I needed for my classes, the reality of my life as a student-athlete started to set in.

I received my class schedule, my football practice schedule, my study hall schedule, my dining hall schedule, my bus schedule—because my dorm was located pretty far from the stadium—and my game schedule. I remember feeling the excitement of all these new opportunities and the weight of expectations all at the same time. How would I juggle my packed schedule, impress my position coach enough that he could convince our head coach to play me in games, do well in school, make it to classes and practices on time, and have a social life? Whether you have yet to experience college, have already been through it, or are now juggling an athletic career, managing all of your commitments can be tough. And if you don't learn how to manage your schedule and deal with all the expectations, it can greatly impact your mental health.

"A large national survey of college students conducted in 2020 (in collaboration with the University of Michigan) found that nearly 40 percent experienced depression. One in three reported struggles with anxiety."[3] Athletes deal with the same levels of stress as all college students, but we also deal with some stressors that aren't always recognized as negative to our mental health. We are taught to have thick skin and brush off negative comments. To just ignore memes about us, social media posts that attack

---

3. Randi Mazzella, "Why Do College Athletes Keep Dying by Suicide?," *Psycom*, January 5, 2023, https://www.psycom.net/student-mental-health/college-athletes-how-to-help.

us, comments that pressure us to be perfect, and media coverage of our embarrassing moments on and off the field. If these things bother you, it's okay to tell someone you trust and talk to a professional about it, as well as limit your media and social media consumption. In fact, it's more than okay to do this—it's necessary.

Death by suicide is on the rise among athletes. "The year 2022 may go down as one of the deadliest in college sports history. In a span of just two months (in March and April), five college athletes—four women and one man—died by their own hand."[4] If this doesn't get our attention, I'm not sure what will.

Your life matters. Your life is worth living, and your obstacles can be overcome. God wants you to know that no matter how tough life gets, he is by your side every step of the way. These are not empty words. However, you need to play a part in this as well. You must believe the words of Deuteronomy 31:8: "The LORD himself goes before you and will be with you; he will never leave you nor forsake you. Do not be afraid; do not be discouraged." God promises to help you through what may seem impossible. Always remember that your life is worth living.

LET'S PRAY

Dear God,
Please give me the strength to overcome obstacles and help me not to stuff my feelings rather than admitting when I'm struggling. Equip me with the humility to seek help when I need it and preserve my mental health. Amen.

POSTGAME KEYS

1. If you are struggling right now, please don't stay quiet. Talk to someone you trust and get help from a professional if you think you need it.
2. If you are considering harming yourself, immediately dial 988, the

---

4. Mazzella, "Why Do College Athletes."

Suicide and Crisis lifeline. Someone is available to talk with you twenty-four hours a day.

3. Your life matters. Your life is worth living. Your obstacles are worth overcoming.

67   DATING GAME

But since sexual immorality is occurring, each man should have sexual relations with his own wife, and each woman with her own husband.
1 CORINTHIANS 7:2

PREGAME

Are you currently dating anyone? What is your purpose for dating right now? Are you interested in pursuing this person to marry in the future?

GAME TIME

In this day and age, dating can be tricky. There are so many depictions of what dating should look like. It's no wonder there is so much confusion surrounding dating. What does the playbook say about dating? And how can we follow it?

When you are interested in someone, you should hold yourself to a high standard. Don't be so desperate to date that you let your standards slip. There are seasons to dating, and you should appreciate each one. First off, don't let anyone make you feel less than because you are single. It's okay to not be in a relationship. Work on yourself and enjoy doing things independently, without worrying about how your decisions and actions may impact a significant other. Enjoy being able to spend countless selfish hours working on your sport and training, trying to be the best version of yourself, playing uninterrupted video games by yourself, and having long prayer and Bible study sessions alone with God.

Eventually there will come a time when a friendship with a special person develops into a romantic relationship and you begin dating with a purpose. Do not date for hookups. Intentionally and gracefully say no to those with whom you don't see a future and say yes to the one you can see blossoming into a future marriage.

We sometimes do things out of order because that's what we see in our culture. We date and barely know the person, then let our flesh be our guide and engage in sexually immoral activities with people who are not our husbands or wives. Sex is beautiful when it's reserved for marriage. But when it's done out of order, outside of marriage, or with someone else's spouse, it can cause many problems and unwanted issues, such as fogging your focus, interrupting your goals, and ruining your future. I've heard many stories about how sex before marriage ruined a good thing. However, for those who are married and having sex within a marriage, it is beautiful, honorable, and good in the sight of the Lord.

If you're already married, continue learning about your spouse, asking questions, listening, and remembering to keep dating each other. The same energy you put into courting and wooing each other should continue throughout your marriage.

Whatever season you're in, take your time, appreciate every moment, don't rush, trust God, and strive to live a pure life. Your eternal life is worth more than a moment of immoral gratification.

LET'S PRAY

Dear God,
Please give me the strength to control my flesh and appreciate the season I'm in. I don't want to settle for less; I want your perfect will for my life. Amen.

POSTGAME KEYS

1. If you are struggling in the purity department, contact a counselor, pastor, or website where you can get help and accountability.
2. Here is a website I recommend: www.covenanteyes.com/2015 /11/05/online-directory-of-sexual-purity-communities.

3. To have a healthy dating relationship, make sure you set boundaries that will keep you safe and pure. Set a curfew for your hangout. Have someone hold you accountable and ask you the hard questions regarding your relationship. And remember to keep God at the center of your relationship.

ESPORTS

Do nothing out of selfish ambition or vain conceit.
Rather, in humility value others above yourselves.
PHILIPPIANS 2:3

PREGAME

Are you a gracious winner? Do you treat both your teammates and your opponents with respect? Do you model good sportsmanship?

GAME TIME

Online gaming is rapidly growing, and it doesn't seem to be stopping anytime soon. Many of us grew up playing video games for fun, but sometimes our tempers would get the best of us because of our competitive nature. In this day and age, gaming is at a completely different level. Local competitions, tournaments, copious training, and thousands of hours of in-game play exist. To be a professional gamer, you need to put in a lot of hours working on your craft.

Esports teams often practice six days a week for six to eight hours per day. That is a full-time job. Most professionals have adopted the mentality that they will eat, sleep, breathe, and dream their game. I personally love video games so much that I started an Instagram account called @mentalbreak.lab, where I get a chance to tap into nostalgia in the gaming world, do unboxings of cool tech, nerd out, and take a mental break here and there. With all that said, I'm nowhere near the level it takes to be an esport athlete. I'm a variety gamer who loves to compete, and who knows? Someday I may take that next step and compete professionally!

I've watched many esports competitions, and, just like any other sport, you see players who demonstrate great sportsmanship and players who have awful sportsmanship. It doesn't matter what you do in life, your character and attitude show how you represent Jesus. As believers, the way in which we are supposed to treat others is countercultural. Most of the time our world highlights and reveres the selfish—those who step on others to reach the top, those who strive to be famous at any cost, those who sacrifice their morals to be seen as the best, and those who will compromise their beliefs to reach the pinnacle of fame and fortune.

As Christians, we are to live our lives as servants. We are to serve our families, communities, teammates, coaches, churches, and anyone else we come into contact with. No matter how you compete—whether it's in traditional sports or esports—you are blessed to play the sport you love. Cherish your position in life, and work to be a blessing to others. Life is short, so make it count and invest in your eternal future by considering your actions today.

LET'S PRAY

Dear God,
Please remind me that I'm on this earth to serve others. Remind me of that when I'm feeling weak and angry, and I'm tempted to react negatively. Amen.

POSTGAME KEYS

1. Meditate on Philippians 2:3 this week and apply it to your daily life.
2. I challenge you to memorize these Scriptures: Romans 12:10 and Mark 10:45.
3. Jesus came to serve. If we want to be like Christ, we must have a heart to serve others. We have to be willing to put others before ourselves. Look for opportunities to help someone specific this week.

69

If any of you lacks wisdom, you should ask
God, who gives generously to all without
finding fault, and it will be given to you.
JAMES 1:5

PREGAME

Do you have new people in your circle who want to be around you? Can you trust your friends? Have you started receiving more and more attention for what you do?

GAME TIME

It's good when the people in your circle are trustworthy, but it's a challenge when some of them only want to be around you if it benefits them. When you're an athlete—especially a successful or high-profile athlete—there will always be people who try to insert themselves into your life so they can be associated with your success. Sometimes, it takes tough situations for you to know who your loyal friends are. Clout-chasers and attention-seekers will do whatever they can to attain the notoriety they crave, but they run away when times get tough and they don't get anything from you.

We must carefully discern those we can trust and those we need to keep at a distance. The wrong people in your circle are like weeds in the garden—they choke out the good plants and take over. Getting rid of weeds can be challenging, but they must be removed because they rob the good plants of nutrients, water, resources, and sunlight. They also occupy space and attract unwanted problems, as do those we shouldn't have in our inner circle.

The wrong friends can create a false sense of entitlement that can get you in trouble.

The wrong friends can stunt your growth.

The wrong friends can bear seeds of insecurity.

The wrong friends can distract you from your tasks and goals, impacting your accomplishments.

The wrong friends can take up too much of your time and keep you from your purpose.

The wrong friends can turn you away from God.

Believe and trust that God will give you the wisdom and discernment to protect your inner circle and allow the right people into your life. As you progress in sports and anything else you do in life, you will need this type of godly wisdom when dealing with teammates, friends, brands, teams, peers, agencies, agents, fans, and so many more who are interested in being a part of your inner circle. Keep a close eye on that circle and ask God for his discernment as you go about your life.

LET'S PRAY

Dear God,
I ask for your wisdom and discernment when dealing with the
people who come into my life. Help me to know which people are
actually for me and which are against me. Amen.

POSTGAME KEYS

1. Reflect on how you feel about your current inner circle, including your family, friends, and people in your life.
2. Pray for God to bring people into your life who are trustworthy and have your back.
3. Ask God to reveal anyone who does not belong in your life and ask him to send the right people to be a part of your life.

70

CHIP ON YOUR SHOULDER

Do not accuse anyone for no reason—
when they have done you no harm.
PROVERBS 3:30

PREGAME

Have you ever been overlooked by a coach, a team, a teammate, or another individual? How did or does it make you feel? Do you feel the need to prove them wrong?

GAME TIME

In sports, we often root for the overlooked players who bring to the game a story of overcoming adversity. Those players who carry a chip on their shoulders sometimes offer a compelling reason to cheer for them, and their story makes for entertaining conversations and interviews. I know it can be a huge motivator to improve and perform at a higher level if you think you have something to prove. When I played varsity basketball as a high school freshman and won a starting role, I had a chip on my shoulder because some people thought I didn't deserve to start over an upperclassman. I was too young in their eyes. However, I wanted to prove them wrong and leave no doubt that my age didn't matter.

The only problem was, I became harder on myself than usual and hyper-focused on perfection and not messing up, which made me quick-tempered, unpleasant to be around at home, and heavily burdened. My dad noticed the change and had multiple conversations with me. He eventually helped me realize I was more focused on what others said about me than on the opportunity right in front of me, which was generously given to me by the gift-giver—God.

I needed to shift the focus off myself and the naysayers and set my sights on Jesus to help lighten the load. People will always have an opinion and something to say. We can't control how they act or what they say. However, we have the ability to control how we respond to our circumstances.

Leave it in God's hands. There is a reason he orchestrated the path you are now on. A closed door in one area is an open door elsewhere. Be thankful God closed that door because he knows it isn't what's right for you right now. Be fully present in your now, let go of dead weight, brush that chip off your shoulder, and trust in God's plan for your life.

LET'S PRAY

Dear God,
Thank you for bearing the weight of my pain, anger, and stress. I
don't want to walk around with a chip on my shoulder. I release my
burdens and give them to you. Amen.

POSTGAME KEYS

1. If you are carrying some heavy burdens right now, stop and give them to God.
2. Focus on Jesus and trust that he controls your situation right now.
3. When you feel angry or feel the need to prove yourself, remember that you have nothing to prove. God has already handled things.

71   LISTEN TO YOUR BODY

Am I now trying to win the approval of human beings, or of
God? Or am I trying to please people? If I were still trying
to please people, I would not be a servant of Christ.
GALATIANS 1:10

PREGAME

How do you know when to play through an injury and when to take time off and let yourself heal? Have you ever felt guilty for not practicing or playing through an injury? Have you ever played through an injury, knowing you shouldn't?

It was a muggy, hot day in Oxford, Ohio, and our team was getting ready for our game at the end of the week. I was having a great practice and feeling quick. On the very next play, the quarterback handed the ball off to me and, as I was reading the defense, the play broke down. I ran to the right side but had to adjust as I approached the line of scrimmage. When I planted my right foot to cut up field, our three-hundred-plus-pound defensive lineman jumped on my back, twisting my body to the left while my foot stayed planted in the turf. Immediately, I felt a shooting pain in my right ankle and knew I'd done something to it. I just wasn't sure what. I grabbed my ankle, and the training staff came over, evaluated me, and took me inside to get imaging.

The imaging revealed that I had a high ankle sprain and would be sidelined for four to six weeks, which wasn't what I wanted to hear. *Can I tape it up and play through the injury? Will I lose my spot? What will my coaches think? Will my teammates think I'm soft because I got hurt? How long will my ankle take to heal completely?*

All my thoughts were about how everyone else would view me. I started to compare myself to other athletes who had endured injuries and kept playing. For example, former San Francisco 49ers safety Ronnie Lott broke his pinky finger in an end-of-season game trying to tackle Dallas Cowboys running back Timmy Newsome. The 49ers were going to the playoffs, and Lott was faced with a decision. Either the doctors would place a pin in the finger, and he would wear a cast while it healed for eight weeks, or he would have the tip of his pinky finger amputated from the first joint up. Ronnie Lott chose to have his finger amputated, and he was able to play the very next week. He was seen as a warrior and a hero. However, in a *Sports Illustrated* article, Lott had this to say:

"I was trying to laugh it off, but I felt sick," he told the AP in 1986 of first seeing the nub. "I tried to stand up, but I broke into a cold sweat. It was just a total shock. I thought, 'Oh, man, I should have had the pin put in.' . . . We are losing the compassionate side of sports. We're becoming gladiators. If I ever become a coach, I hope I never lose sight of the fact that players are people. They feel. They have emotions. I could have all of Eddie DeBartolo's corporations and it isn't going to buy me a new finger. It has given me a new perspective on life."[5]

It's easy to compare ourselves to others and lose sight of reality. We all want to please our coaches, teammates, and others, but we cannot lose sight of who we ultimately need to please. When we live our lives to please God and we make it a priority to stay connected to him, he will give us the spiritual wisdom to make the right decisions, including knowing when to say no, knowing when to say yes, and knowing what our bodies are telling us. Don't make big life decisions based on money, coaches, or others. Consult with God, and trust that he will give you the strength and wisdom to make decisions that will be the best for you and bring him the glory. Listen to your body, and, ultimately, listen to the Lord.

LET'S PRAY

Dear God,
Please help me listen to my body and not compare myself to others
or try to please the world. I want to be in your perfect will for my
life, and I want to listen to you. Amen.

---

5. Robert Klemko, "Ronnie Lott's Amputated Pinkie Finger," *Sports Illustrated*, June 17, 2014, www.si.com/nfl/2014/06/17/nfl-history-in-95-objects-ronnie-lott-amputated-pinkie-finger.

1. Listen to your body and take care of it, and don't be guilt-tripped into doing something you know you shouldn't. Don't jeopardize your future to please the world.

2. We should constantly want to please God. It's not always easy, but these Scriptures are great reminders: 2 Timothy 2:15 and 2 Chronicles 7:14.

3. There is life after your sport, so ask yourself, *What do I want my quality of life to be? How do I want to live my life after I can no longer play my sport at a high level?*

72   WORK HARD

Do everything without grumbling or arguing, so that you may become blameless and pure, "children of God without fault in a warped and crooked generation." Then you will shine among them like stars in the sky.
PHILIPPIANS 2:14–15

PREGAME

Would you consider yourself a hard worker? What does hard work mean to you?

GAME TIME

My AAU basketball coach loved telling us we were the best-conditioned team on the court, no matter who we played. That was a bold statement to make because he couldn't possibly know how well-conditioned every other basketball team was. However, he was confident in how he conditioned us, and he didn't take any flak for it. If you spoke negatively about him, another coach, or a teammate; complained under your breath about the work he made you put in, you wouldn't play in the next game—and that would be your only warning. You'd be dismissed from the team if you did it again.

In Philippians 2:14–15, "grumbling" refers to negative emotions, discontent, and complaining about things you don't like. Don't be the person who complains about workouts, practices, expectations, training camp, minicamp, preseason training, or off-season training. You are the standard, and you are a representative of Jesus. You are a leader, and if you hide this Scripture in your heart and live by it, you will be a shining light for your teammates, coaches, community, family members, and fans.

Unfortunately, nowadays it's rare to find people who live by this code and have a strong work ethic. Inspire those around you with your positive attitude and determined work ethic, and when they ask you why you are so different, you can tell them it's because of Jesus in your life. Tell them, "I couldn't be this way if it wasn't for him." Work hard—and then point back to Jesus.

LET'S PRAY

Dear God,
I want to be a light in this dark world. Help me to appreciate life
and the opportunities I have been given and not to complain about
working hard. Amen.

POSTGAME KEYS

1. Write down Philippians 2:14–15 and post it in your locker, your room, or a place where you can see it as a daily reminder not to grumble about what you need to do this week.
2. List a few things you complained about recently, and ask God for forgiveness. Then throw the list away as a symbol of no longer complaining about those things.
3. When you work hard, you will see the fruits of your labor. Meditate on Psalm 128:2 this week.

73

I do not run like someone running aimlessly; I do not fight like a boxer beating the air. No, I strike a blow to my body and make it my slave so that after I have preached to others, I myself will not be disqualified for the prize.
1 CORINTHIANS 9:26–27

PREGAME

Do you make it a priority to pray daily? When was the last time you hung out with God? Do you make time in your day to study your Bible?

GAME TIME

Paul likened an athlete's way of training and preparing for their sport to how we live the Christian life. The two are very similar. When you train, you practice with a goal in mind and play with a purpose. You don't aimlessly work out in the gym without having a plan of attack. You don't condition your body without knowing what you're working for. You follow a strategic protocol for your success. In the same way, we need to live the Christian life with purpose—because God has a purpose for us.

As athletes, we constantly beat our bodies into submission through training to become stronger, more resilient, quicker, and better skilled. As Christians, we do the same thing when we live our lives with self-control. You become stronger when you can control the urges of your flesh and not give in to the world's way of operating. Your endurance as a Christian will constantly be tested and strained. The more time you spend with God in worship, prayer, and Bible study, the more you will become like Christ. We should aim to be more like Christ daily. When it is time to meet God, we want to hear him say, "Well done, my good and faithful servant. You have fulfilled what I placed you here on earth to do." How incredible will it be to hear that one day?

Enjoy your sport, play with purpose, and have fun while doing it. It's a gift. At the same time, don't forget to enjoy spending time with God, learning in faith, and having fun while spreading the good news. Just as practice and training are necessary for your athletic accomplishments, prayer, worship, and devotion are necessary for a strong relationship with Jesus. Live with purpose and live for the Lord.

LET'S PRAY

Dear God,
I want to live purposefully and not walk around aimlessly, wast-ing time. I pray that my relationship with you grows stronger as I intentionally spend time with you. Amen.

POSTGAME KEYS

1. Spend a certain amount of time every day connecting with God. If this is your first time doing this, start with five minutes. Each week, add another five minutes until you reach a reasonable amount of time you can stick to.
2. Being married to consistency will greatly impact your intentional walk with the Lord. Try to keep a consistent schedule.
3. Be aware of things that waste your time. For example, monitor how long you spend on your phone swiping through social media, dating apps, video games, or streaming movies and shows for hours. Give yourself a limit and stick to it.

74 RESPECT EVERYONE

Show proper respect to everyone, love the family of
believers, fear God, honor the emperor.
1 PETER 2:17

How do you treat your teammates and coaches? Do you have respect for them? Are you able to listen to them and learn from them?

As a rookie or a new player on the team, you should always do your best to talk less, ask more questions, and pay more attention. If you are willing to pick up the gems of wisdom your coaches or elder teammates are dropping, you can learn so much.

I understand there are instances when certain players or teammates can rub us the wrong way, and it's hard to treat them with respect, especially when they are not being respectful. However, we are supposed to be the example of what it looks like to display Christian love to others. If we can love others, even those who are hard to love, we honor God, which pleases him and results in a blessed life for us.

I once watched a player disrespect a stranger's property in public, and it was hard for me and my teammates to respect him after the incident. Several of us were walking to an event, and he felt the need to try to impress us. "Do you dare me to jump through this car window?" he asked. No one took him seriously, but the next thing we knew, he sprinted toward the parked car, jumped into the air with his knees tucked to his chest, extended his legs forward, and launched himself into the car, breaking the window in the process.

I couldn't believe my eyes. Why would he damage an innocent person's vehicle and cut up his legs in the process? All for what—to impress us? He was older and supposedly wiser than us. Yet he made a major mistake, and it would make sense that others would lose respect for him. There is a standard for human beings when it comes to respecting others and their property. As a Christian athlete, you are to be an example to others who are watching you. When we respect, listen to, and follow God, we can be assured he will never lead us the wrong way.

Dear God,
Help me find ways to show respect for the people you have put in
my life—my teammates, coaches, friends, and family. Remind me
that you love all of us and help me show that love to others. Amen.

POSTGAME KEYS

1. Ask yourself this question: *Would the world be able to tell that I'm a Christian by my actions toward other people?*
2. Your obedience to God will help you treat everyone with respect.
3. Make a list of people you can show better respect to today, this week, this month, and this year.

YOU ARE MORE

See what great love the Father has lavished on us, that we
should be called children of God! And that is what we are!
1 JOHN 3:1

PREGAME

What do you do for fun outside of your sport? Do you have any hobbies? What brings you joy when you're not practicing or competing?

GAME TIME

Hopefully, you enjoy the sport you get to play. Some of us love our sport so much that we eat, sleep, and breathe soccer, swimming, baseball, cross country, wrestling, martial arts, cricket, volleyball, golf, surfing, archery or whatever sport you play. We are obsessed with the game and every part of it. Sometimes, that obsession can affect our lives outside of athletics. If you are having an amazing time winning and are experiencing success, you are probably in a great mood. However, if you are not playing well or are dealing with negativity, it can begin to impact your personal life.

You are so much more than your sport. You are an incredible human being with gifts and talents that far exceed the sport you play. You are a child of God. Your identity is rooted in Christ, who is the foundation in your walk with him. When you keep Christ at the forefront of your life, you begin to realize that whatever you're involved in—your vocation, extra-curriculars, sports, comes second. You are not defined by how well or how poorly you play. You will experience blessings in both the wins and losses of life because both are necessary for your growth as a human being.

If you're an athlete, it's healthy to have other outlets in life that bring you joy. If you are creative, tap into that aspect of yourself. You can make music, draw, read, start a podcast, or play video games. Take the time to do what you love. Do you like to go on hikes, experience nature, hang out at the beach, do puzzles, or serve at community events? If these things bring you joy, do them!

You never know if you will have to stop playing the sport you love before you want to. It's impossible to know what the future will bring. If your entire identity is wrapped up in sports, you will have a hard time adjusting to something new once your athletic career ends.

Remember, you serve a perfect Father who loves and cares for you more than any human will ever love you. He cares about the desires of your heart, your mental health, and your eternal future. If you're having a hard time figuring out who you are outside of your sport, take the time to search your heart and ask God to reveal more of who he created you to be.

=== **LET'S PRAY**

Dear God,
I don't want to live a life where my identity is fully wrapped up in my sport. I am more than my sport, and I want to find out more about who you created me to be and what I'm to do on this earth. Amen.

1. Write out a list of things you love to do.
2. Make time to participate in those different hobbies or try out different activities if you haven't yet found your thing.
3. Have a conversation with God about your life and its direction. Share your heart, and then take time to be silent so you can hear from him. Give God the chance to speak to you.

76 · SO MUCH TO BE THANKFUL FOR

Thanks be to God for his indescribable gift!
2 CORINTHIANS 9:15

What are you thankful for? Is it easy for you to find things to be grateful for? Or is it hard for you to see the blessings in your life?

With the way negativity is often highlighted in our world, it's sometimes hard to see our blessings. Do you notice that when someone does something great, you hear about it, but as soon as they do something negative, it appears to wipe out all of the positive things they accomplished? Success can be so fleeting in this world.

I have the privilege and honor of addressing 70,000 fans at Lumen Field for Seattle Seahawks home games on any given NFL game day. The feeling is exhilarating. The energy that comes from the 12s (Seahawks fans) is unexplainable. I'm grateful for every chance I get to step onto the field and speak to our fans, and I never take it for granted. The opportunity to bring joy to a fan base, to make people smile, and to help them feel seen and loved is my mission. God didn't have to open this door for me to walk through, but he knew it would be a perfect fit and would bring me incredible joy.

Likewise, 2 Corinthians 9:15 can remind you that you have so much to be thankful for.

You are blessed to be alive as you're reading this right now. Not every one of your friends has made it this far in life. Think of how blessed you are to play the sport you love. The sport you play and the doors it will open for you might change your life. Not everyone has the opportunity to use their athleticism to impact other people's lives for Jesus Christ. God didn't have to give you the abilities he gave you. Please don't take your life for granted or compare your journey with anyone else's. You are uniquely created with a purpose and skill set that God wants to use for his glory.

LET'S PRAY

Dear God,
Thank you for breathing life into my lungs and allowing me to be used by you today. Lead me and guide me in your ways. Order my steps and remind me of how blessed I am to be in the position you have put me. Amen.

POSTGAME KEYS

1. How do you think God is using you right now? As he reveals your area of service, recommit to staying faithful to his purposes for your life.
2. Memorize 2 Corinthians 9:15, and write it on your cleats, shoes, or anywhere else you will see it.
3. Start a team gratitude journal to help create a positive atmosphere and mindset for your team. Encourage anyone on the team to write something positive before or after each practice.

77

BE AVAILABLE

Submit yourselves, then, to God. Resist the
devil, and he will flee from you.
JAMES 4:7

Do you make yourself available to God? Have you told him that he can use you? If God doesn't have your heart, what does?

You better be available when your coaches call your name, or you can miss an opportunity. If I stood on the sidelines or sat on the bench during a game, I made sure I was close enough to hear the coach call my name. I always wanted to be available with my time and talents. I always wanted to take advantage of opportunities to play. I would have been upset with myself if I'd missed the coach's call and not been able to enter the game.

Can you imagine working hard all your life, putting yourself in a position to be drafted by a pro team or chosen for your country's Olympic or national team, and then not making yourself available? I watched a friend of mine almost miss an opportunity he dreamed about and worked for his whole life—an NFL career. The team was on the clock and called his phone to tell him he was drafted. However, due to bad service, he did not receive their call. The only notification he had was a missed call. He called back, but he was only able to reach the front desk, where nobody answered. The panic started to build, a cold sweat washed over him, and his stomach knotted up. He felt the anxiety of his NFL dream not becoming a reality—and all because he thought he missed the call.

Thank God, the NFL team was finally able to connect with him and draft him in the final few seconds, but it was panic time up until then. Panic is what we should feel if we do not make ourselves available to God. He wants us to submit our time, talents, and obedience to him. But, in reality, God cares more about availability than ability. When we are available and obedient to God, he makes the ordinary in our lives extraordinary. He puts the super in our natural, and success follows our obedience.

=== LET'S PRAY

Dear God,
I want to be used by you. I don't want to be distracted by the ene-
my's tactics and miss my opportunity to make a difference in this
world. Thank you for always being available to me. Amen.

=== POSTGAME KEYS

1. Make sure you are always willing and available to be used by God.
2. Position yourself next to God so you will hear him calling you to get in the game.
3. Can God rely on you to be available to be used by him in any area of your life?

78   OUR LIFESTYLE

But if anyone obeys his word, love for God is truly made
complete in them. This is how we know we are in him:
Whoever claims to live in him must live as Jesus did.
1 JOHN 2:5–6

=== PREGAME

Does your lifestyle glorify Jesus Christ? What comes to mind when you think of Christian living?

 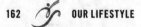

When I started playing sports, I played because I had a genuine interest and love for the game. As I got older and became more seasoned, I added new reasons for why I played those sports. I wanted to be great. I wanted to play at the Division 1 level and eventually go on to play in the pros. It wasn't until high school that I started wanting to glorify God with my lifestyle as an athlete. I began to read my Bible more, listen more carefully at church, pay better attention during Bible studies, and ask my dad and mom—who were both pastors—more and deeper questions about what I read about Jesus.

As I read the Gospels, I studied how Jesus treated others and made note of how he responded to temptation, trials, and tribulations. Jesus always made sure God was at the center of everything he did. That is how we are to operate. We are to bring glory to God by keeping him at the forefront of our decision making, words, and actions. We glorify God by practicing and playing to the best of our abilities.

When you call yourself a Christian, you are part of a special family and team, and God is your coach. Your actions on and off the field directly reflect who you serve. Believe it or not, your decisions and actions can minister to or mislead people who are watching you. When your focus is on living a life that is pleasing to the Lord, your lifestyle will reflect the Jesus in you and may inspire others to begin a journey of finding out what makes you so different.

LET'S PRAY

Dear God,
I want to live a life that is pleasing to you. Please rid me of behavior
that isn't pleasing to you. I want to represent you to the best of my
abilities by being open to receiving your guidance. Amen.

POSTGAME KEYS

1. Your lifestyle as a Christian athlete should represent the God you serve.
2. Write down some ways you can treat your teammates, opponents,

referees, and friends with the same love and respect God gives to you.

3. Ask God to help you be sensitive to the Holy Spirit and to discern when your lifestyle starts to waver. Be open to humility and guidance so you can stay on track.

79 FIGHT OPPOSITION

"If the world hates you, keep in mind that it hated me first.
If you belonged to the world, it would love you as its own.
As it is, you do not belong to the world, but I have chosen
you out of the world. That is why the world hates you."
JOHN 15:18–19

PREGAME

How do you feel when people do not like that you are a Christian? Do you tend to play down your beliefs, or do you make sure others know you follow Jesus?

GAME TIME

One early morning at a Young Life camp where I was serving as a leader after college, our cabin went on a morning mountain bike ride. We were given instructions about our bikes, the trail, and safety precautions. Then, we started on the trail and zipped down the mountain. Some of us had GoPro cameras attached to our helmets to capture footage of the ride.

I was having so much fun when suddenly, I hit a rocky and technical part of the trail. I slowed down a bit because I didn't want to crash or, worse, go over the side of the mountain. As I squeezed the brakes, my bike tipped forward and stopped abruptly, sending me flying like Spider-Man Miles Morales when he jumped off the building for the first time in

Spider-Man: Into the Spider-Verse. My limbs flailed everywhere as I headed right for two trees. I mustered up enough athleticism to twist my body so I missed one tree and banged my shoulder into the other, which braced my fall and kept me from completely going over the side of the mountain.

On that mountain bike ride, I was moving forward on a path, but I still had to deal with opposition. That is what it's like to live as a Christian in this world. Living for Jesus will not be easy when you're dealing with different worldviews, conflicting standards, opposition, and disrespect for what you believe. You can get knocked down and discouraged when you live your life counter to the culture. You may live in this world, but you don't belong to this world.

Dealing with opposition here on earth is worth it because we get to experience eternal life in heaven. Be strong, be courageous, and know that your role right now is critical as God uses your influence, actions, and lifestyle to tell others about his goodness. Fight the opposition and stay on the side of the Lord.

LET'S PRAY

Dear God,
Please protect me while I share the gospel in this world. Help me
not to have a spirit of fear. Give me strength and courage as I live
my life for you. Amen.

POSTGAME KEYS

1. If we have a relationship with Jesus, we will deal with opposition in this world.
2. We are to be unapologetic about our relationship with Jesus, even if it's tempting to keep it private and not draw attention to ourselves.
3. Think of people in your life who can help you with your Christian walk, and stay connected to those people. If you weren't able to think of anyone, seek out a couple people who can be that kind of support to you. Don't go through life as a Christian alone.

DON'T BE HARDHEADED

Stop listening to instruction, my son,
    and you will stray from the words of knowledge.
PROVERBS 19:27

Is it hard for you to be told what to do? How do you deal with being disciplined?

When I was a youth pastor, I loved spending time with the kids in our youth group. We had many athletes attend, and it was an honor to speak into the kids' lives and support them in their extracurricular activities. There was one baseball player who was naturally talented but wanted to do things his way. He thought he could get away with not listening to instructions because he was really good. He started drinking a little alcohol here and there, which turned into smoking weed every now and again, which escalated into taking hardcore drugs. We tried to warn him and get him help, but he refused to listen to the people who cared about him. Eventually, an untimely overdose claimed his life. It was extremely sad to watch him turn his back on his friends and coaches, make poor choices, and ruin his life.

God places people in your life who will help you along your journey. These people can include your parents, coaches, pastors, mentors, good friends, and even Bible study leaders. We need to pay attention to the people God has put in our lives to guide us. Neglecting their wisdom and instruction is essentially saying you would rather gamble with your life, and that is a dangerous way to live. Only Jesus had it all together.

We need wisdom, we need instruction, we need direction, and we need humility. All of these things can save us from pain, stress, anxiety, death, and destruction.

Wisdom can keep you on the team.

Wisdom can get you more playing time.

Wisdom can keep you safe.

Wisdom can get you through doors no man can shut.

Wisdom can help keep you quiet when you need to be.

Wisdom can keep you out of trouble.

Staying on God's path is hard when you rely on yourself. Trust the Lord to bring the right people into your life to help you with your journey so you don't wander aimlessly through this world. Don't be hardhearted—keep your heart open to God's instruction and guidance.

LET'S PRAY

Dear God,
I humbly ask for your wisdom and guidance. Speak to me through your Word as well as through those who possess your wisdom. I don't want my attitude or my ignorance to hold me back from living my life for you. Amen.

POSTGAME KEYS

1. Meditate on these Scriptures to remind you how to deal with constructive criticism: Proverbs 12:15 and Proverbs 4:7.
2. God places people in your life who will help you along your journey. Don't isolate yourself from them.
3. Don't believe everything you read or hear about you. Take time away from social media if needed. And meditate on these words of Jesus: "I am leaving you with a gift—peace of mind and heart. And the peace I give is a gift the world cannot give. So don't be troubled or afraid" (John 14:27 NLT).

*I waited patiently for the L*ORD*;*
     he turned to me and heard my cry.
He lifted me out of the slimy pit,
     out of the mud and mire;
he set my feet on a rock
     and gave me a firm place to stand.
He put a new song in my mouth,
     a hymn of praise to our God.
*Many will see and fear the L*ORD
     and put their trust in him.

PSALM 40:1–3

PREGAME

How is your mental health? How are you doing with everything you are juggling in your life right now?

GAME TIME

I want to take a moment to remind you that your mental and physical health need to be treated with equal amounts of care. When we struggle with a physical injury, a trainer or doctor evaluates our symptoms to see if we are okay. If we aren't, we do whatever it takes to address the situation and start healing. When we struggle with our mental health, we may tend not to take it as seriously and overlook the symptoms, which can be dangerous. Our feelings and emotions can become overwhelming and spin out of control if we don't tend to them.

Admitting you battle mental health issues is not just okay; it's totally normal. It is admirable—and important—to be honest about what you are dealing with. Struggling with your mental health is nothing to be ashamed of, and you are certainly not alone. Take it as seriously as you would a physical injury. When you notice something is off, seek help immediately.

In the Bible, Elijah went through a tough time in his life. First Kings 19:4 reads, "He himself went a day's journey into the wilderness. He came to a broom bush, sat down under it and prayed that he might die. 'I have had enough, LORD,' he said. 'Take my life; I am no better than my ancestors.'" You may not be in Elijah's exact headspace, but his mental state didn't just happen. It started somewhere.

Mental health issues might start subtle—a quiet pain that "isn't a big deal" or feelings stuffed down because it doesn't seem worth the effort to deal with. When you notice something is wrong and doesn't get better, talk to a mental health professional, coach, pastor, mentor, or family member. Don't put it off or tell yourself that it will go away on its own. Your mental health is critical to your well-being and overall success. You are too important to ignore it.

God is faithful and can bring you out of your rough patch. In turn, your story can bless others who have similar struggles. But first, you have to be self-aware and reach out for help. God believes in you. He is always here, willing and waiting to lift you up out of your suffering.

LET'S PRAY

Dear God,
Thank you for caring about my mental health. If I need help, lead
me in the steps I need to take to become whole again. Amen.

POSTGAME KEYS

1. Your mental health is every bit as important as your physical health. Pray and assess where you're at. Know that it's okay to get help.
2. If you battle mental health issues, the most important thing to do is to tell someone. Don't stay silent. If there isn't anyone in your life you feel comfortable talking to, you can call a mental health

hotline. Search *mental health hotline* on the internet and reach out for help.

3. Search for Bible verses that offer comfort and remind you of God's love for you and his promise to strengthen you and help you. Start with these—Psalm 9:9–10; 34:18; 56:8; Isaiah 41:10—and know that God is always with you.

COOK EVERYTHING AND EVERYBODY

I can do everything through Christ, who gives me strength.
PHILIPPIANS 4:13 NLT

PREGAME

What is your mentality when you prepare for a game? How do you approach practice?

GAME TIME

You should approach every practice, game, match, fight, or event with a mentality to dominate. God wants you to play to the best of your abilities, which takes preparation, focus, and appreciation of your opportunity and skill set. When you are at practice, you should attack your duties as if competing for a championship. Whoever tries to stop you from scoring, winning, or doing well, you have to cook them and make them think twice about their efforts to be great. When they compete against you, they should be second-guessing their devotion.

I'm not saying you should be rude, disrespectful, or unruly. But if you take your craft seriously, you should play or train at an elite level in every practice—not just when you're competing. Work on becoming mentally strong and fearless. Train your body to be physically strong, elusive, mobile, flexible, quick, and fast. This high level of preparation will set you up for success in your competitions. You will not feel like you need to step up your game when you compete, because you already operate at a high level in everything you do, from practice to individual workouts, open gyms to pickup games.

Paul is saying in Philippians 4:13 that if we rely on God for strength and not on ourselves, he can help us do everything. God will give you the strength to endure through any circumstance. You may second-guess your ability to overcome situations, but when you rely on God, he always blesses your hard work and appreciates when you give your all to be the best you can be, even when your competition ends in a loss. Beautiful life lessons can be learned in defeat that will make you better, stronger, and more strategic and experienced in the future.

Your maximum effort and hard work—if they're for the right reasons—will honor God. If you want to be great, you must work, trust God, make sure Jesus is at the center of everything you do, and cook everything and everybody in your path. This means you must outwork your opponents, train with excellence, compete with integrity, refuse to let distractions knock you off your course, and never settle for less.

LET'S PRAY

Dear God,
I don't want to have a spirit of fear. Help me to work hard, and
when it's time to battle, please calm and ease my nerves. Also
remind me that it's fun to do what I get to do—especially when I've
put in the effort and get to experience the rewards. Amen.

POSTGAME KEYS

1. You have nothing to fear when you compete. God is with you and for you, and he will bless your hard work.
2. Write down everything you are fearful of—old injuries flaring up, not being prepared enough, the ability of your opponent—and ask God to remove them. Trust that if you've done the work, God will take away your anxiety so you can play to the best of your abilities.

3. Here are a couple Scriptures to read and speak over yourself: Psalm 23:4 and Psalm 27:1.

MAKE TIME

Look to the LORD and his strength; seek his face always.
1 CHRONICLES 16:11

PREGAME

Do you make it a priority to spend time with God every day? Is it easy for you to go days without spending time with him? What happens when you forget to connect with God?

GAME TIME

Sometimes ignorance is bliss. I used to get on airplanes and walk by the first-class seats, glance at them, and wonder, *What's the big deal?* They didn't seem much different from the other seats on the plane, other than the fact that you had more room. Plus, if you chose to sit in the emergency seats and were willing to help the flight attendants if anything went wrong, you had a lot of leg room. I didn't see why anyone would spend extra money on them. Until I experienced them for myself.

I was flown out for a speaking engagement, and the organization booked first-class tickets. I was extremely thankful that they would bless me in this manner, but I really didn't understand the difference. As soon as I sat in my seat, the flight attendant approached me and asked, "Would you like a drink and a snack?" I thought to myself, *This* is *different!* In coach, you are in the air for a while before flight attendants walk down the aisle with their carts, offering passengers their choice of a small beverage and toddler-sized snacks. Not in first class. There, you choose from soft-baked chocolate chip cookies, full bags of chips, warmed-up nuts, and a warm, damp cloth to wipe your hands with. I didn't even know that warmed-up nuts were a thing. They were delicious. I was like a kid in a candy store, playing with the gaming controller for my screen, and laying my seat back like a bed. Who knew?! Since then, I've flown coach plenty of times, but I now know what I'm missing, and I appreciate flying first class so much more when I do have those opportunities.

Sometimes, when it's been a while since we've spent time with God, we forget what we're missing. There have been seasons of my life I went long periods of time without opening my Bible. Just because I didn't read the Bible during that stretch of time didn't mean I wasn't a Christian any longer, but it still affected me. When you go long periods of time without that connection to God, you feel it in your life. You tend to react to situations rather than respond kindly and gracefully. You tend to have a shorter fuse, and your convictions get diluted. Your spiritual compass is in disarray.

Before you met Jesus, you didn't know how much you needed him in your life and how much of an upgrade life with him is. After you experience the goodness of God, it's like flying first class—except for your whole life, not just the length of a flight.

LET'S PRAY

Dear God,
Help me fall in love with your presence. Heighten my desire to
spend time with you daily. Thank you that life with you is so much
better than life on my own. Amen.

POSTGAME KEYS

1. If it's been a long time since you last talked to God, stop what you're doing and spend time with him.
2. Find a Bible-reading schedule that you can commit to.
3. Read these Scriptures this week: Psalm 34:8 and Lamentations 3:25–26.

84 YOU NEED VISION

Where there is no revelation, people cast off restraint;
> *but blessed is the one who heeds wisdom's instruction.*
PROVERBS 29:18

What are your goals? Do you have a vision for your life? Do you have a vision for your season?

When I was growing up, depending on the season, my dad took us to local sports games, track meets, and boxing matches, and occasionally, when he could, he took us to college football games. Plus, we watched all types of sports on TV. Both of my parents did martial arts, and we watched all of the Bruce Lee movies, as well as the film *The Last Dragon*, which starred an actor named Taimak, who became my childhood hero.

My parents exposed my brother and me to many different sports, paying attention to what we gravitated toward. We were into martial arts, boxing, soccer, football, basketball, and track, but football and basketball became our favorites. I dreamed of playing in the high school games my dad took us to see, then playing on Saturdays on a D1 football team. I dreamed of cutting down the nets after winning an NCAA basketball championship.

Before my games, depending on what season I was in, my dad had me close my eyes and visualize myself running the plays our team had practiced, so that when I was in the game, it would feel familiar. I played running back in high school, and I vividly remember envisioning myself running a play called thirty-two trap, breaking through the line of scrimmage and bouncing to the right side of the field and scoring. That Friday night, during my game, the offense called thirty-two trap. It was the weirdest yet coolest feeling when I was given the ball. It felt as though that moment had already happened. I ran to the scrimmage line, and as one of my blockers fell, I had to react and bounce it to the right side. Then I streaked up the right sideline and scored. In that moment, my vision became reality.

Having goals and a vision for our lives is great, but without divine guidance, we will aimlessly roam the earth. Visualization in our sport can be a powerful tool, but our sport is only one aspect of our lives. We need to have an overall vision for our lives, one that is directed by the architect of life. Without vision and direction from God, we won't know when to say yes or no. God gives us a vision for our lives, including the sports we play and the decisions we make.

LET'S PRAY

Dear God,
Please give me your divine guidance and show me a vision for my
life. I want to live my life from a kingdom perspective. Help me to
follow your vision. Amen.

POSTGAME KEYS

1. Write down all of your goals and dreams. After you are done, pray and ask God how they fit into his vision for your life.
2. Take time to remember past situations God has helped you through, which will help you discern whether you are hearing from him in the present.
3. Let Scripture guide you to align with God's vision for your life. Proverbs 16:3 and Proverbs 3:6 will help you with your decision making.

85

But when God, who set me apart from my
mother's womb and called me by his grace, was
pleased to reveal his Son in me so that I might
preach him among the Gentiles, my immediate
response was not to consult any human being.
GALATIANS 1:15–16

PREGAME

Would you consider yourself special? Do you feel weird answering that question with a yes? I'll answer it for you: You are absolutely special!

GAME TIME

So often, we believe the things others say about us. People like to label us, thinking they know who we are. But they don't see us from God's point of view. If we live to please the world and make others love us, we give people—not God—the power to determine our self-worth. Have you ever looked in the mirror and said, "I wish I could change my nose, my ears, my eyes, my body, my hair, my lips, my teeth, my height, my skin tone . . ."? But that's not how we should look at ourselves. God doesn't make mistakes. You are uniquely made, and you are a gift to this world.

Many of us are so concerned about being loved and accepted that we give everyone around us permission to evaluate our self-worth. As an adolescent, you might sacrifice your own identity to get the attention of others. You might deny yourself food so you can lose weight and try to fit the "ideal" image sold by social media, ads, and the entertainment industry. You might listen to what your peers say someone should look, act, talk, or dress like. Even as adults, we buy the myth that our appearance is our number one asset—one that will bring us acceptance and approval from others. Eating disorders abound, people turn to plastic surgery and steroids to alter their appearance, and insane amounts of money are spent on clothes, shoes, cosmetics, and more.

You are not what people say you are. You are who God says you are. The Bible reveals in Ephesians 1:4–5, "For he chose us in him before the creation of the world to be holy and blameless in his sight. In love he predestined us for adoption to sonship through Jesus Christ, in accordance with his pleasure and will."

God wants us to find our identity in him. Don't worry about trying to please the next person at the expense of your peace. It's not worth it. God made you unique—a special design. You are chosen.

LET'S PRAY

Dear God,
Thank you for choosing me and creating me as a special vessel
for you. Please help me never forget my worth and to see myself
through your eyes. Amen.

POSTGAME KEYS

1. Ephesians 2:10 says you were created for a purpose: "For we are God's handiwork, created in Christ Jesus to do good works, which God prepared in advance for us to do."
2. When you need to remember God is in control, remember Romans 8:31: "What, then, shall we say in response to these things? If God is for us, who can be against us?"
3. Write a list of your insecurities on a piece of paper. Be completely honest. Once you've written them down, offer this prayer: *Lord, I give these insecurities to you, renew my mind, and remind me of how you see me.* Then throw the list away or burn it in a firepit, and believe that the way you view yourself is renewed in Christ.

USE WISDOM

Be very careful, then, how you live—not as unwise but as wise,
making the most of every opportunity, because the days are evil.
Therefore do not be foolish, but understand what the Lord's will is.
EPHESIANS 5:15–17

What is your process when it comes to making decisions? How do you choose your friends, what events to go to, who to hang out with?

I was invited to many parties when I was in college. I knew I had to be careful with which ones I attended and which ones I turned down. I did end up going to some parties I shouldn't have, where I could have gotten into a lot of trouble—or even lost my life. During my freshman year, one of the first college parties I attended was at a club in a sketchy neighborhood. I rode over with some teammates and when I got there, I felt in my spirit that I shouldn't be there. However, I didn't drive to the party, so I was at the mercy of the upperclassman I'd ridden with.

As we entered the club, the music was loud and the place was packed. About an hour into the party, a fight broke out in the middle of the dance floor. Bottles were thrown, fists went flying, and hair was pulled. My friends and I located each other to ensure everyone was okay, and we headed outside. As soon as we cleared the door, gunshots rang through the air. We sprinted quickly to our car and fled the scene. My heart was pounding in my ears, and I remembered the feeling I had when I entered the club. It was the Holy Spirit warning me, but I didn't listen. I'm so thankful God protected us that night, but I don't want to constantly take chances and miss out on prompts from the Holy Spirit.

When we connect daily with God, we become familiar with his voice.

Satan will try to distract you, set traps for you, and put you into compromising situations that could ruin your life. That's why it's so important to seek God's wisdom. In Ephesians 5:15–17, Paul reminds us that we must be careful how we live our lives. As Christians, we must use wisdom to make decisions about what we participate in, where we go, and who we hang out with. Base your decisions on the Holy Spirit's guidance and God's wisdom, and you'll never get off-course.

LET'S PRAY

Dear God,
I want to include you in every area of my life, and I want to make
wise decisions. Please continually speak to mé through the Holy
Spirit, and please keep me safe. Amen.

POSTGAME KEYS

1. Get in the habit of praying about every decision. When you include God in every part of your life, you won't be steered wrong.
2. Pay attention to the small, still voice inside you. That is the Holy Spirit leading, guiding, and speaking to you.
3. God cares so much about you that he makes his wisdom available to you. Seek it out—and use it!

87 FRESH START

I will give you a new heart and put a new spirit in you; I will remove
from you your heart of stone and give you a heart of flesh.
EZEKIEL 36:26

PREGAME

Have you ever felt as if you needed a fresh start? Do you ever wish you could start something over?

We hear it all the time: *New year, new you.* I'm sure you've read a post or heard from someone about what they plan to do to start the new year fresh. I've done it plenty of times myself. I have set goals to level up my fitness, build my business, and spend more time with God. Some years, I followed through and made strides in fulfilling those goals; other years, I was making the same goals a year later. It can be frustrating to fail, but that's likely because we lack the discipline, consistency, and patience to continue what we started. This is human, but there is a solution.

Maybe you have been dealing with anger issues, doubt, tough relationships, bad grades, poor decision-making, addiction, lack of motivation, or unanswered prayers. Maybe you've transferred schools or have been traded to a different team. No matter what your situation is, you want to start fresh. God can help you with this. It begins with your desire to change from within, but don't try to do it on your own. Ask God to help you with your plan of action. Ask him if it's aligned with what he has for you. It never hurts to consult with the Creator of your life on which direction you should go.

It took God's help to free the Israelites from their wicked ways and hardened hearts. When we're worn down and discouraged, staying faithful and positive can be a challenge. If we don't keep our hearts aligned with God, the circumstances of life can rob us of our joy, leading us into a dark space and dimming our light.

If you are in a place where you feel burdened, discouraged, depressed, and unmotivated, and you want to be free from those negative emotions, God can help you. He can help you hit your life's reset, refresh, and reboot buttons; renovate your heart; and restore your joy, inspiration, and zeal for life. He will give you a new heart and a new spirit, and you can start fresh today.

LET'S PRAY

Dear God,
I want to start fresh with my goals and dreams. Please soften my
heart and renew my mind to be free from today's troubles and my
past burdens. Help me to run all my plans by you. Amen.

1. You can start fresh at any time. Just call on God and ask for his help, and then have the faith to walk in the newness of life he brings.
2. If you need to rededicate your life to Christ, you can do it right now. Just repeat this prayer: "God, I want to start fresh today and rededicate my life to you. Please forgive me of my sins. I want to commit my life, actions, heart, and mind to you today. Amen."
3. When you start fresh, here are a few Scriptures to encourage you and give you confidence in your new journey: 1 Corinthians 13:11 and Galatians 2:20.

OWN YOUR SCHEDULE

Teach us to number our days,
that we may gain a heart of wisdom.
PSALM 90:12

PREGAME

Do you wish you could be better at time management? Do you want to be productive, but you tend to procrastinate and wait until the last minute to finish a task?

GAME TIME

Can you relate to assuming you have plenty of time to get a project or assignment done until your deadline is looming and you still have a lot to do? That put-it-off mentality used to get me in trouble all the time. During my senior year of college, my professor gave me a generous time frame to work on my senior thesis. The deadline seemed far in the future, and I felt like I had plenty of time to work on it, so I put off thinking about it for a while.

As the end of the year approached, I realized I needed to lock down and give my energy to my senior thesis, because I felt myself getting senioritis. Graduation was a few months away, and post-graduation life was becoming real. My family made plans to attend my graduation ceremony and throw me a graduation party. By this time, I knew I was moving to San Diego, which, for an Ohio kid, was extremely exciting. However, none of those plans mattered if I didn't finish my senior thesis, because that would mean I couldn't graduate.

Why do so many of us do this to ourselves? I used to say that I thrived under pressure and was clutch, and that's why I waited until the end to finish something. I relished the feeling of always coming through and getting things done at the last minute. Although part of that was true, the other 85 percent was poor time management skills, energy spent on unnecessary stress, and lack of wisdom. In the grand scheme of things, our time on this earth is very short. God wants us to maximize and be good stewards of our time. We must own our days and walk in wisdom. Making godly choices applies to how we manage our lives—and how we manage our time.

God doesn't want us to waste our time and procrastinate. We have real goals, jobs, and responsibilities we need to take care of, and if we own our schedules, we can be more efficiently used by God. I became more successful when I learned how to own my schedule and appreciate the time God gave me on this earth. You may want to be more or do more in life, but God wants to see you be faithful with little before he blesses you with much.

LET'S PRAY

Dear God,
I want to respect the time you bless me with. Please help me to manage my time well and not put things off so I can do all you have created me to do. Amen.

1. There are a lot of books you can read to help you have better time management skills. A few of my favorites are:

   ▶ *The 7 Habits of Highly Effective People: Powerful Lessons in Personal Change* by Stephen R. Covey
   ▶ *Atomic Habits: An Easy & Proven Way to Build Good Habits & Break Bad Ones* by James Clear
   ▶ *Deep Work: Rules for Focused Success in a Distracted World* by Cal Newport
   ▶ *The 80/20 Principle: The Secret to Achieving More with Less* by Richard Koch
   ▶ *Getting Things Done: The Art of Stress-Free Productivity* by David Allen

2. If you want to have more opportunities to be used by God, own your schedule. This is your moment to choose to be efficient with the time God has given you.

3. Time is precious. Here is a Scripture to remind you of that truth: Ephesians 5:15–17.

89   BE CONSUMED

Jesus answered, "I am the way and the truth and the life. No one comes to the Father except through me."
JOHN 14:6

Do you feel like you have a real relationship with God? If not, how can you develop your relationship with him?

When you are romantically interested in someone, you want to spend a lot of time with them. The same goes for hobbies and sports we love. When I meet other athletes, I can always tell which ones love the sport they get to do. Their consuming passion for their sport is obvious when they talk about it. They study the little things. They geek out on the history of their sport. They can talk about their sport for hours on end.

This kind of passion shows an appreciation of the game and a consuming fire within to give it their all. It's something that teammates, coaches, and fans love to see.

As Christians, we are to have that same passion for Jesus. The Creator of the world wants to spend time with you, and we should feel the same way about him. I pray that your heart desires to learn who Jesus is, how he thinks, and how he lived while he was on earth. I pray you will be consumed with learning everything there is to learn about Jesus.

I pray that when you open up the Bible, you will have a burning passion for hiding the God-inspired Scriptures in your heart, longing to be filled to the brim and overflowing with the love Jesus has for humanity. We are so blessed that we can give so much to the sport we love—every day we have the opportunity to give it our all. Imagine giving God your all, putting him first and applying his teachings to your entire existence.

When you follow Jesus and are consumed by him, you will have an unfair advantage over those who don't have Jesus in their lives. Your life will have meaning and purpose. You will have favor with God and man, because your actions and lifestyle will be pleasing to the Lord. Do yourself a solid and open your Bible daily, pray every day, worship God often, and follow the Lord with faith.

LET'S PRAY

Dear God,
I want to really know you. Reveal yourself to me daily and help me to give my all to living life for you. Amen.

1. Read your Bible slowly. Study it like you study your sport. Take time to observe what is being said and how you can apply it to your life.
2. Spend time in a Bible study to learn together and share what you're learning.
3. Find an accountability partner to help you stay motivated and prioritize spending time with God. Coaches help us stay accountable in our sport, and we need the same support to grow in our relationship with God.

HIGHS AND LOWS

There is a time for everything,
and a season for every activity under the heavens:

a time to be born and a time to die,
a time to plant and a time to uproot,
a time to kill and a time to heal,
a time to tear down and a time to build,
a time to weep and a time to laugh,
a time to mourn and a time to dance.

ECCLESIASTES 3:1–4

PREGAME

How do you respond to change in your life? What are some of the hardest changes you have had to navigate?

GAME TIME

I was feeling good about my performance in the track meet at that point. I had won the 100-meter race and placed first in the long jump, but I still had the 200-meter race and the 400-meter relay left. When it was time to run the 200, I warmed up and got into my blocks to set up for the race. In the moment when the crowd goes quiet and the runners wait to hear the starting pistol, there is a feeling of peace, nervousness, and anticipation. I always loved that moment.

Bang! The gun went off, and I exploded out of my starting blocks. I sprinted the curve and felt great. I was in my sweet spot, and I knew that when I came out of the curve, I would turn it up a notch and sprint all the way through the finish line. As I started to power out of the curve, I felt a pop in my hamstring and immediate pain shot through my leg. I had to pull up, hopping on one leg. Just like that, my day went from a high to a low.

That can be life sometimes. You can experience a great moment and then suddenly encounter a rough one. You will go through ups and downs in sports, school, relationships, and everything else. But during the ups and downs, God doesn't want you to panic. He wants you to have poise, have faith in him, and remember he is with you through every season. Friends, family, situations, and environments may change, but Jesus stays the same. Hebrews 13:8 tells us, "Jesus Christ is the same yesterday and today and forever."

Always have confidence that God is by your side, and you will make it through the highs and lows of life in this world.

LET'S PRAY

Dear God,
I know that seasons come and go. Give me the strength to stay
even-keeled, cool, calm, and collected through the ups and downs
of life. Amen.

POSTGAME KEYS

1. How are you handling the season of life you are in right now? Write out your feelings and pay attention to them. Make a habit of doing this as you navigate the changing seasons of your life.
2. If you feel shaken, disturbed, or bothered in the season you're in,

ask God for his peace, which surpasses all understanding. If the changes seem too overwhelming or if you're dealing with several changes all at once, don't hesitate to reach out and ask for help.

3. One of the most comforting characteristics of Jesus is that he will not change. Memorize Hebrews 13:8, and it will give you peace.

91   THE FIGHT IS NOT YOURS

You will not have to fight this battle. Take up your positions; stand firm and see the deliverance the LORD will give you, Judah and Jerusalem. Do not be afraid; do not be discouraged. Go out to face them tomorrow, and the LORD will be with you.
2 CHRONICLES 20:17

PREGAME

Do you feel as if you have something to prove? Do you ever get involved in a battle that isn't yours to fight?

GAME TIME

We put unnecessary stress on ourselves when we try to prove our worth to others. We sometimes take ourselves—and what others think or say about us—too seriously. Don't be afraid to minimize your pride so you can maximize your joy and security. If there is less of you and more of Jesus, you will feel less stress to prove yourself.

Second Chronicles 20:17 shows us how to respond as Christians during moments of stress or crisis. We need to bring every problem and out-of-control situation to the Lord. God wants you to know that through his strength, you will prevail. You have a choice: fight your battles on your own or fight them with the strength of our mighty Father.

Giving it to God and believing he will go before you and fight on your behalf is the better route. We deal with so many issues in our lives—identity, racism, sexism, politics, discrimination, mental health, and so many more. Trying to fight every battle on our own is exhausting.

There is power in refusing to engage in conflict. The fight is not yours; give it to God and let him battle for you.

LET'S PRAY

Dear God,
I submit my pride to you. I submit all of my battles to you. Help me
to be humbler and wiser when I feel like I have something to prove.
Amen.

POSTGAME KEYS

1. When you're tempted to get involved in an argument or a fight, remind yourself that God is in control and he will be there for you in all situations.
2. Second Chronicles 20:17 is a life-changing Scripture I encourage you to memorize. Maybe even write it down and post it in a place you can read it daily.
3. When someone angers you, and you feel tempted to snap back, take a deep breath instead, walk away from the situation, and pray.

92 STUMBLING BLOCKS

Therefore let us stop passing judgment on one another.
Instead, make up your mind not to put any stumbling
block or obstacle in the way of a brother or sister.
ROMANS 14:13

PREGAME

How do you respond to being made fun of? Does it bother you, or can you dish it back in fun?

There was a teammate of mine who loved to crack jokes and clown everybody on the team. It didn't matter who you were, you were not safe from being one of his targets. He could dish it out, but he could not receive it. He would joke about someone else and have the locker room howling in laughter, but the minute someone clapped back and clowned him, he took it seriously and was ready to throw blows. He alienated himself from the rest of the team because he wouldn't hesitate to tear people down, but he became incredibly sensitive—and angry—when the verbal mirror reflected back on him.

We should always consider how we speak to others. I love banter, having fun with my friends, cracking jokes, and getting made fun of, but you must pay attention to your heart even when you think you're just having fun. We used to hear people say, "Sticks and stones may break my bones, but words will never hurt me." However, this statement is false. Our words carry a lot of weight—they can hurt others and become stumbling blocks and damage our lives.

We ultimately want to lift people up with our words. We should be ambassadors of empowering, elevating, and encouraging dialogue. Have fun with your teammates, family, friends, but make sure you discern what you can and cannot say to certain people. At the end of the day, you must answer to God for your words. Use them wisely, and don't cause anyone to stumble.

Dear God,
I want to be an agent of harmony. Help me watch what I say to
others so my words are not stumbling blocks to others. I want to
build people up rather than tear them down. Amen.

1. You can either lift others up or tear them down with your words. Be sensitive to everyone around you and watch what you say.

2. Think of a way you can build someone up with your words today.

3. The teams and organizations with the best chemistry have the best chance of success. Let Romans 14:13 be one of your mission Scriptures for you and your team.

93   HEALER

The LORD sustains them on their sickbed
and restores them from their bed of illness.
PSALM 41:3

PREGAME

Do you believe God is a healer? Have you experienced healing in your own life? Have you known someone who was healed from injury or sickness?

GAME TIME

It was January 2, 2023, week seventeen of the NFL season. I was watching the Buffalo Bills play the Cincinnati Bengals on TV in my living room. It felt like a normal Monday Night Football game, and I was excited to watch those teams battle it out. With about five minutes left in the first quarter, Tee Higgins ran the ball, dropped his shoulder, and hit defender Damar Hamlin in his chest. Damar tackled Tee down to the ground and then popped up to his feet. But moments later, he suddenly collapsed on the field. At the time, viewers had no idea what exactly had happened as medics rushed to his side and performed CPR on his body. Later, it was revealed that he suffered cardiac arrest.

It was a scary sight and tough to watch. Prayers started to circulate all over the media and social media, and I watched ESPN analyst Dan Orlovsky pray for Damar on live TV. Despite the scary circumstance, it was incredible to see people worldwide come together and lean on God for his healing power. No one knew Damar's condition, how he was doing, or if he would pull through. But people had faith and asked for God's healing power to restore him to health. Matthew 18:20 says, "For where two or three gather in my name, there am I with them." And that's what was happening.

Today, we can look back and see how incredible God is. He is our healer when we are sick or injured. He nurses us back to health, and he knows what we need. He brings restoration to our bodies. In times of trouble, we can rely on our faith and God's healing power. Romans 8:28 says, "And we know that in all things God works for the good of those who love him, who have been called according to his purpose." God is the great healer, and we can trust in him.

LET'S PRAY

Dear God,
Thank you for the countless number of people you have healed.
Help me have more compassion for people and pray for them to be
healed, knowing you can do it. Amen.

POSTGAME KEYS

1. Here are some Scriptures to have in your tool belt if you need healing. Repeat them over yourself or someone else.

   Heal me, LORD, and I will be healed;
       save me and I will be saved,
         for you are the one I praise. (Jeremiah 17:14)

   He heals the brokenhearted
       and binds up their wounds. (Psalm 147:3)

   And the prayer offered in faith will make the sick person well;
   the Lord will raise them up. If they have sinned, they will be
   forgiven. (James 5:15)

2. Create a list on your phone or in your journal of people you will commit to pray for this year. This is one way to serve others and be part of the process and blessing that is taking place in their lives.

3. Memorize Matthew 18:20: "For where two or three gather in my name, there am I with them."

CLASS ACT

Humble yourselves before the Lord, and he will lift you up.
JAMES 4:10

Would you consider yourself a class act? Who do you admire as a class act? What do you think the term means?

Generally, someone who is a "class act" is regarded as impressive, humble, poised, well-mannered, confident, and polite. They're a person who lets their actions—rather than their words—speak for them. There aren't too many of them out there and when you encounter one, it is refreshing.

I was so impressed when I watched a standoff between two incredible fighters—Terence Crawford and Errol Spence Jr.—who were getting ready to go head-to-head on one of the biggest stages. Instead of getting in each other's faces and mean mugging, talking trash, or creating a spectacle, these gentlemen—a.k.a. class acts—thanked each other for making the fight happen. They dapped each other up with respect and love, despite the fact they'd enter the ring the next day and battle each other like gladiators. They truly gave off grown, mature, humble energy. There was a graceful confidence about them and the way they interacted with each other.

James 4:10 reminds us that God resists the proud, haughty, arrogant, conceited, bigheaded people of this world. We are to live humbly, display gentleness, and represent Jesus with our lifestyle. And if we humble ourselves to the Lord, he will lift us up. God will open doors no man can shut. Humility is attractive to God and results in more of God's grace in your life. He will place you in positions and places you can't even imagine because he knows he can trust you. When you are a class act, God knows he will be well represented by you.

The accolades you achieve and receive will not leave this earth with you. Acquiring fame, fortune, clout, and name-brand possessions won't get you into the gates of heaven. That's why you need to live your life with Christ in mind. Do you serve Christ, or do you serve man or self?

I'd rather be a class act and look good in the eyes of the Lord than try to impress people with hollow actions that burn up on judgment day.

LET'S PRAY

Dear God,
I want to be a class act, representing you everywhere I go. Keep me humble and gracious and remind me to keep you as number one in my life. Amen.

POSTGAME KEYS

1. Can you think of someone you know who is a class act? List their best attributes, and then try to model them yourself.
2. Humility is attractive to God, and God uses humble people to carry out his plans.
3. To be a class act, you must be kind, humble, and care more about other people than you care about yourself.

95

TIME TO STAND UP

Finally, be strong in the Lord and in his mighty power. Put on the full armor of God, so that you can take your stand against the devil's schemes. For our struggle is not against flesh and blood, but against the rulers, against the authorities, against the powers of this dark world and against the spiritual forces of evil in the heavenly realms.
EPHESIANS 6:10–12

PREGAME

Is it easy or tough for you to stand up for what you believe in? Are you unapologetic about your relationship with God? Do people know what you stand for?

GAME TIME

I was at the gym working out with some of my friends, and after our lift, we went into the basketball gym and shot around for a while. While we were shooting, one of my friends asked me a question out of thin air: "Why are you so happy all the time?" I looked at him and started to laugh. I said, "First of all, I can't let you believe I'm always happy. I have days when I'm not." He replied, "I know that, but the majority of the time, you are always smiling, and to be honest, it makes me question why I seem to be the opposite."

I said, "Well, do you really want to know?" He said, "Absolutely." I told him the secret to my happiness was Jesus in my life. I couldn't be this way or find this much joy in my life if it wasn't for Jesus. Then, I said I know I'm here for a reason, and I'm thankful for what God has saved me from. The next thing my friend said was one of the coolest responses I've ever heard. He told me he was an atheist, but my faith seemed genuine. That conversation opened the door to other conversations about Jesus over the next year. To this day, I don't know if my friend gave his life to Jesus. But I do know that a seed was planted, and maybe he will encounter someone else who will water it and see it bloom.

I want to encourage you to keep learning who Jesus is. Let his guidance to you in Scripture and your time spent talking to him in prayer build up your confidence in him. We need to put on the armor of God in order to fight correctly. This battle we are up against is spiritual. The enemy knows your weaknesses and will try to exploit them or break you down.

The enemy wants to distract you from experiencing God's goodness, because he knows he doesn't stand a chance against God and his warriors. The thought of a generation of athletes growing closer to God and unapologetically sharing their faith is powerful, and the idea of it weakens the enemy's knees. Draw closer to God. Imagine the lives you can impact with the goodness of God through your brave actions and truthful words.

LET'S PRAY

Dear God,
Give me the strength and boldness to stand up for you without fear.
When others ask me about the source of my joy, help me to answer
truthfully and tell them that it all comes from you. Amen.

POSTGAME KEYS

1. If you are a Christian but have been hesitant to share your faith with others, ask yourself why, and ask God to remove that fear so you can walk in boldness.
2. I am reminded of Ephesians 6:10–12 daily, because it's tattooed on my arm. I want you to tattoo this Scripture on your heart. Speak it over yourself daily.
3. Here are a few Scriptures to help you be bold in your faith: Psalm 27:1 and Romans 8:31–32.

No one is like you, LORD;
*   you are great,*
*   and your name is mighty in power.*

JEREMIAH 10:6

Do you believe God is great? How do you see his greatness show up in your life?

One day when I showed up at my job as a youth director, I was called into my boss's office. He sat me down and praised my talents and great attributes. Then he dropped the bomb: "You don't fit here." He told me that while he thought my job wasn't a good fit for me, he did believe I was called to ministry. He even told me he would make a few phone calls to set up an interview for me elsewhere, where he thought I would be a better fit.

None of it made sense, but I was determined to trust in God. I told him, *God, you are awesome, and I know you have a bigger plan for my life. I will trust in you.* I asked God to help me not react in the moment. I asked him to prevent me from telling my boss what I was thinking in my head. I was hurt and angry, but I didn't want words spoken in the heat of the moment to be used against me or block my blessings. I told my boss just the day before that my wife was pregnant with our fourth child, and then he turned around and let me go from my job without a real explanation.

The news spread quickly, and many of my coworkers were furious. Some of them even wanted to go to human resources and file a complaint. However, I knew I needed to gather my thoughts, pray, and wait to hear from the Lord. I needed to trust in his bigger plan for my life.

When we are let go from a job, treated unfairly, traded to another team, forced to transfer, or caught off guard, it's so easy to speak the language of fear. We worry about how we will be able to pay our bills, buy groceries, or pay rent. If it's related to our athletic career, we wonder if we should stop playing the sport we love. In this particular situation, our family didn't know how our bills would be paid, but we chose to speak life.

God, you are a good God who will provide for our family.

God, you will supply all of our needs.

God, you are with us in this tough time, and we will be anxious about nothing and not have a spirit of fear.

Sure, I had some moments alone with God where I voiced my anger and pain, but I did not abandon my faith in how great God is. And he came through for our family. All of our bills were paid, and we were blessed to make a cross-country move that turned out to be a major blessing in disguise. When facing trials, don't speak fear; speak life, speak faith, and trust that God will see you through. One day, your story may be a testimony that will bless thousands or tens of thousands of people.

LET'S PRAY

Dear God,
Thank you that you didn't give me a spirit of fear. You made me
strong, hopeful, and full of faith. You have equipped me with a
sound mind. Help me to remember that you are great and can do
all things. Amen.

POSTGAME KEYS

1. There is no one in history like our God. He is the King of kings and Lord of lords.
2. If there is anything you are fearful of, speak life over it right now and remember you serve a God who is great and can do all things.
3. God is almighty, powerful, all-knowing, loving, and caring, and he wants the absolute best for us. Meditate on Psalm 104:2.

Do not be deceived: God cannot be mocked. A man reaps what he sows.
GALATIANS 6:7

PREGAME

Are you rude and disrespectful to others, or do you treat them with kindness and respect? How do you expect other people to treat you?

GAME TIME

You are sowing the seeds of your future by the things you do and say, and the way in which you treat other people. The word *sow* means to plant seeds with expectations of growth. The decisions we make now can directly impact our future. If we commit crimes and get in trouble, we serve prison time. If we bully others or treat them with disrespect and then one day need to rely on those people, they may be hesitant to help us. If we sow laziness in the classroom and get bad grades, we pay the price by which schools we are—or are not—eligible to attend.

What are you sowing for your future today? Do you sow hard work in the classroom, in the weight room, and on the practice field? Do you treat others with compassion, appreciation, empathy, and encouragement? Or do you treat them with disrespect, impatience, disdain, and judgment? Do you talk negatively about others? Whatever seeds you scatter is the harvest you will reap. You need to ask yourself, *What would I like to see bear fruit in my life?* The answer will guide you in the decisions you make today.

If you're uncertain about what to do in any situation, you can always ask God for his wisdom. James 1:5 reads, "If any of you lacks wisdom, you should ask God, who gives generously to all without finding fault, and it will be given to you." Remember that you reap what you sow, so make sure the seeds you sow in your life are ones that will have a positive effect on your future.

Dear God,
I want to sow only good seeds in my life. Please forgive me for the
bad seeds I've sown. From here on out, help me to sow only good.
Amen.

1. Write out a list of ways you can sow good seeds (examples: honor your parents, speak kindly of and to others, be generous, pray for others).
2. Be careful how you treat people and what you post online and on social media. It really can be a small world.
3. Read Proverbs 22:8 and Galatians 6:7–8 to understand the importance of the actions you are sowing.

---

98   MISSION POSSIBLE

Jesus looked at them and said, "With man this is
impossible, but with God all things are possible."
MATTHEW 19:26

Has anyone said you are not good enough? Do you have people in your life who doubt your capabilities? Who do you turn to when you need someone to pump you up?

Some of my peers said I was not good enough to play football or basketball for a Division 1 school. They said our high school was too small and I lacked exposure. During my senior season, our football team went 1–9. That was extremely tough to go through as a competitor. Most people didn't see the countless hours of hard work I put in behind closed doors. While my peers were partying, sleeping, and not taking their craft seriously, I was training, studying film, critiquing my mistakes, learning from other D1 athletes, and going to camps to showcase my athleticism.

Although I lived in a small town and attended an even smaller high school, God had my back. All it took was going to the Ohio State Buckeyes football camp my junior year, where I was able to show my abilities to the university coaches. I caught their eye, and the seemingly impossible became possible. Others may have doubted me, but someone never did—God. And he loves to make the impossible happen for those who love and follow him. When we focus on God and not on the things of the world, we leave room for God to work on our behalf.

Every day, you have choices to make. You can choose to be swayed by the insecurities of people in your life. You can allow their negativity to talk you out of what God has placed within you and to deter you from where God is taking you. Or you can trust God, put him first in your life, and be the best version of yourself by giving your best effort. When you do this, you can trust God to open the doors that need to be opened, and you'll be okay with the doors God closes, because you know he does everything for your good.

LET'S PRAY

Dear God,
Please help me remember that all things are possible with you. I want to live a life that demonstrates my faith in you. Help me focus on you and not the world as I follow my goals. Amen.

POSTGAME KEYS

1. No matter where you are in your life, stop and focus on God and acknowledge that he can make the impossible possible in your life.
2. Commit Matthew 19:26 to memory and recite it when times get tough.
3. Write down some ways you can demonstrate that you believe all things are possible with God by your side.

WHO IS JESUS?

I and the Father are one.
JOHN 10:30

When you hear the name Jesus, what does that name mean to you? What role does Jesus play in your life? Is Jesus real to you?

Jesus was born from a young woman who was a virgin, named Mary, and God was his father. This made him both God and man. He was God in the form of man when he was here on earth. According to John 1:14, "The Word became flesh and made his dwelling among us. We have seen his glory, the glory of the one and only Son, who came from the Father, full of grace and truth."

Jesus is love. Jesus is holy. Jesus is the Prince of Peace. Jesus is our redeemer. Jesus is Lord. Jesus is our Creator. Jesus is the Son of the living God. Jesus is the head of the church. Jesus is a prophet. Jesus is the author and finisher of our faith. John 14:6 says, "Jesus answered, 'I am the way and the truth and the life. No one comes to the Father except through me.'"

Jesus was God's ultimate sacrifice to wipe away our sins and give us a chance at eternal life. That's where we come in. We are to share the good news with as many people as possible, which is our primary purpose on this planet as Christ's followers.

As Christian athletes, we have such a precious responsibility. Through our platforms, abilities, personalities, and love for others, we can be ambassadors of Jesus and invest in our eternal salvation by being obedient to the word of God and bring others to know him. Being a *Christian* means you believe in Jesus Christ and reflect him through your life and actions. May you become more and more like him.

Dear God,
I believe you came to this earth as both God and man in order to
fulfill your purpose and give us a chance at eternal life. Use me as
an ambassador for you and help me to tell more people your good
news. Amen.

1. Jesus was both God and man when he was here on earth.
2. We are God's ambassadors to share the good news and win souls to Christ before he returns. This means sharing with them the word of God and letting him do the work of drawing them to himself.
3. I challenge you to care less about what others think of you and more about their eternal salvation. You can start now with how you live your life. Just be ready when people have questions about why you are different. Let them know Jesus Christ changed you.

100 GROWTH MAY TAKE SEPARATION

Walk with the wise and become wise,
*   for a companion of fools suffers harm.*
PROVERBS 13:20

How do you get better at your sport? What steps can you take to improve? How can you learn more about God and grow in your relationship with him?

I used to play one-on-one basketball against my younger brother in our driveway. The games were intense, competitive, and physical. We went at it for hours. Over time, I started playing one-on-one games against guys older than me. They were more skilled than me, and playing against them challenged me to get better. I knew that if I only played against people I knew I could beat, I would never improve my game or reach my full potential. You should never be satisfied with being the best player on the court if you can find another court and play against better competition.

This is the same mentality it takes for you to grow spiritually. What type of company do you keep? Are you part of a church or small group where you are growing in your relationship with God? If you are being challenged and learning a lot and you're not the one feeding everyone, that is a great place to be. If you are being fed and getting nourished, you're in the right place.

Just like we should desire to level up our athletics, we should also desire to level up our relationship with God. If our circle consists of unmotivated, lackluster athletes and Jesus-illiterate troublemakers, we must reevaluate our companions. We need to be aware of our surroundings and always seek improvement in reading the Scriptures, studying the Bible, and applying God's wisdom to our lives.

You may need to find a new Bible study if you aren't growing in your current one. You may need to find new friends if the group you hang out with is not living for God. Pros take their game seriously. And followers of Christ don't play around when deepening their relationship with Jesus.

LET'S PRAY

Dear God,
I want to always keep growing in my relationship with you. Help
me to know when I need to level up—in sports, in life, and in my
walk with you. Amen.

I don't ever want to take for granted all of the life experiences I've been through, both good and bad. They have shaped the man I am today and inspired me to write this book from every fiber of my being. I wish I had this book when I was in college.

I want to thank everyone who helped shape, support, and inspire me to write this book. If your name isn't in here and you played a part, you know who you are, and your humility in not being named is admirable.

To my mom, Deborah Dooley, thank you for being a mother who supported me and all of my athletic endeavors. Thank you for going to so many of my games and practices. You're an amazing mom.

To my dad, Tom Dooley, who introduced me to sports and was the superhero I looked up to. If not for my dad, I would not have loved sports like I do today.

To my brother, Allen Dooley, thanks for all the intense one-on-one competitions in EVERYTHING.

Lewis Shine II, I'm excited we are living out some of our conversations from Peabody Hall in college. We love sports and continually push each other to impact the world of sports.

Seattle Seahawks, thank you so much for embracing me into the family and inspiring me to go to greater heights, think differently, and always be a man of good character.

Kathleen Ortiz, thank you so much for believing in me. I'm so grateful I have you on my team. You make things happen, and I appreciate you.

Barnes & Noble in Totem Lake, Kirkland, Washington, thank you for the hospitality to write in your store.

Finally, I want to thank the amazing team at Zondervan, who has supported me incredibly. Carolyn McCready, you are one of the most kindhearted people I have encountered. Janna Walkup, I appreciate you. Katie

Painter, this book had to happen. Thank you for being among the coolest sports fans and great minds I know. Devin Duke and Paul Fisher, you guys are incredible at what you do. I am forever grateful for this opportunity and don't take it lightly. I look forward to more in the future.

Building a Family of Faith

Simple and Fun Devotions to Draw You Close to Each Other and Nearer to God

Andy Dooley

Whether your family has been doing devotions for years or you're doing them as a family for the first time, *Building a Family of Faith*—featured on GMA3—is just what you need to help your family connect with one another, grow in faith, and learn how physical activity can influence your relationships and your faith.

Who better to guide you than Andy Dooley—a passionate leader, pastor, social media influencer, fitness professional, and father of four who has worked with families for more than eighteen years through sports, fitness, and ministry.

In this family-friendly devotional, he will help you simplify yet enhance your family's quality time with devotions that children of all ages will enjoy and learn from. As you read through this devotional each week, your family will . . .

- Engage in meaningful conversations through the powerful stories and guided questions about God's Word
- Enjoy physical activities to get your family moving and having fun together
- Value a vibrant prayer life and learn to pray together as a family

Take the weight off your shoulders, and let this fun, easy, and inviting devotional help you build a family of faith.

Available in stores and online!